THE RELUCTANT

PSYCHIC

D TEALER

Copyright © 2017 by D Tealer
Publisher: D Tealer
ISBN: 978-0-9850231-1-9
All rights reserved.

Cover illustration: Martinez D
Chapter illustrations: D Tealer/ Peter Furian/ petalax/ kysha/ Darla Hallmark/ lady-luck/ Audrey design/ strilets/ blueringmedia/ safaravector/ Sergy Shenderovsky

Without permission from the author, reproduction of this book, in any form, is prohibited. The only exception would be by a reviewer, who may quote short excerpts in a review.

Disclaimer: opinions, observances, beliefs, experiences and viewpoints contained in this book are strictly the opinions, observances, beliefs, experiences and viewpoints of the author and do not reflect or represent the tenets or policies of any one person or organization, religious or secular, in any capacity unless otherwise expressed.

Printed in the United States of America

In memory of a beautiful spirit,

Mrs. Pearl B. Ellis
1923 – 2015

Enjoy the Universe!

First and foremost, the intention of this book is not to steer anyone away from current beliefs. Rather, it is an effort to continue creating an environment of broadmindedness and appreciation for varying ideas, experiences, and thought processes.

Some names have been changed to respect those who wish to remain anonymous or due to the sensitive nature of the experience.

CONTENTS

Preamble   XI

1 MY WORLD   1
My Third Eye 6
A Reluctant Psychic 10

2 WHAT DO YOU BELIEVE?   14
Life 16
Fear/Relative Sanity 17
Energy 24
Dreams 28
Whispers in the Dark 35
Protective Forces 45

3 PSYCH-ISM 101   50
Dimensions 52
Time and Space Travel 54
Out-of-Body Experience 57
The Mind vs The Brain 59
Life After Death 61
The Psychic Network 64
Abilities 72
Authenticity 73
Is The Whole World Psychic? 78

4 FAMILY AFFAIRS   83

The Mist 85
Pet Spirits 89
Ghost Busting 91
Spirit Cleansing 94
The Shadow 98

5 SPIRITS IN MY MIDST   102

Prayer 104
A Séance 114
A Second Séance 124
Spirit Guides 127
Revelations and Premonitions 130
Past Life Regression 153
A Final Farewell… maybe 155
Soulmates 159
Epilogue 160

PREAMBLE

I believe that supernatural occurrences and psychic abilities are more commonplace than we would sometimes like to recognize. Fear of the unknown, as well as environmental taming, has been cause for many to ignore ghostly appearances and discount inexplicable events. As we are unable to transcend the mental and emotional capacity of what we have convinced ourselves can (or cannot) exist, it becomes easiest to say it just isn't so. Although the truth is that, it is.

I, too, have had my time of ignoring the enormous powers of the universe, along with my own abilities to commune with them. Growing up in an era when children could ask few questions, in my immediate circle, there were no explanations for the images and information fluttering through my mind. Conversations about spirits, and communicating with them, wasn't viewed as eclectic. It was thought of as *crazy*. So I lived with the gnawing feeling that I was in the wrong space, living in a wrong time, with people who, every now and then, looked at me apprehensively. To lessen this inner struggle of knowing what, it seemed, I should not know, I gradually immersed myself into a more usual way of living. Adapting to a more customary view of my environment, I participated in normal conversations, with seemingly normal-minded folks, becoming as ordinary as I thought I should be. I realized, however, much later in life, that this resolved nothing. The spirits, and my penchant towards the supernatural, would never go away.

For many years, I dawdled through life, searching for my place in the world. It had become increasingly clear that my psychic propensity was not a trait to share with everyone. Not everyone could relate. And I didn't understand it myself. Through the media, psychic ability was portrayed as a joke, nothing real. Later, there were books but, again, no one to help piece together my connection to any of it. My only solution was to forget about it. By 1983, I had established a quasi-normal life. I had married, had children, and, because it seemed a less hectic environment to raise a family, moved from my home state of New Jersey, southward. In 1986, I accepted a position as a police officer, driving myself further from the world of spirituality.

Law enforcement was the perfect arena to continue resisting the energies darting in and out of my life. During the course of my nearly twenty-three year career, just as the environment demanded, I recreated myself into an indifferent character, viewing life from a very different perspective. Whisked away into this foreign belief system, I was encouraged to disbelieve everything that wasn't accompanied with indisputable proof. It was a structure that insisted I believe in nothing and trust in no one. Anything without physical evidence was invalid. To assist in surviving the quagmire of life's dark side, my agency issued me all police accoutrement: a 92F Beretta semi-automatic handgun, one baton, a pair of handcuffs, a canister of pepper spray, and a bulletproof vest. Training in tactics of survival made me mentally ready. Mile runs up and down Porter Road made me physically ready. *Yes, Sir!* No one, however, offered precautions to safeguard my soul.

It has been a gradual and interesting passage back into this world of spirit, filled with rousing experiences and self-revolutionary insights. Having recognized the significance of my journey, so that time would not cloud my memories, I began a journal. Which became my way of providing a level of *proof*. This, along with correspondence with others, has allowed me to maintain the integrity of my recollections.

Now retired, I have shed layers of spiritual misdirection from my mind. I have painstakingly learned the necessity of releasing anxieties and the beauty of allowing life to unfold without interruption. Though still humanly flawed, I have developed an appreciation for the constant challenge of accepting who I am, just as I am.

While I claim no profound relationship with life and all of its intricacies, I do know that there is far more to *being* than I can ever fathom. And so, with no statistics for you to ponder, and more questions than answers, this book simply elucidates my findings of life and its mystical mechanisms. My hope is that, as I share with you my spiritual growth, you can uncover your own.

1 MY WORLD

My curiosity of psychics and such did not develop because of any direct exposure. Quite the contrary. Probably similar to your own neighborhood, I lived amongst normal clusters of working class people, surrounded by logic and practicality. There were communal rules, always enforceable by the community. This meant there were, indeed, mandates. Children were to refrain from lying, stealing, fighting, or cussing, and any deviation from these proper codes of conduct could be expeditiously corrected by any witnessing adult. All of whom insisted on having a say in whatever occurred in our neighborhood.

Through constant interaction, we created our own system of kindness, the quintessence of the spirit of the block: people helping people. Older children walked younger ones to school. Mothers fed dinner to any hungry child. And building superintendents provided sweet treats from the neighborhood ice cream truck to children whose parents could not afford the extravagance. Yet, as neighborly as we were, there was never any direct talk of spirituality. Specifically, there was never any open discussion on paranormal activity.

Paranormal: what is not scientifically explainable.

I am mystified as to how I have come to possess this ability to communicate with spirits. I am unaware of any brain trauma that could have created this condition. There is no analysis deeming me extraordinaire and no generational passage of mysterious information from old, dusty books, filled with spiritual secrets waiting to emerge. Only in recent years have I found that my paternal grandmother possessed the ability to predict future events. Unfortunately, she met with her demise long ago, taking answers to our mutual truth with her. And so, to quell my insatiable inquisitive nature, I continue to search for other views and perspectives. Conducting my own researches through the years, I probe for answers to my questions on life and death, attempting to become clearer about what is really going on in the spirit world, the in-between world. I am pleased with my evolution, though it has rarely gone any way I would have planned.

I was born in the late 1950s in Newark, New Jersey, to an African American father and a Japanese mother. I went home from St. Barnabas Hospital into a *project* housing development (a topic for another discussion) on Boyd Street. Occupied primarily by residents of Black America, it would now accommodate my Japanese/Black American family, as we sprinkled ourselves into the mix. While we were not the only family of varied ethnic heritage, we certainly were not the majority. Further diversifying my existence, my mother converted from Catholicism to Nichiren Buddhism before I reached the age of four. With these cultural and religious variances, my views of the biosphere, and people within it, was often unlike those of my contemporaries. Then, there was my proclivity to *see*.

Prior to my matriculation into kindergarten at the 18th Avenue branch of the Newark public school system, I had a quiet and easy life at home. While my older brother was off to school, and our mother busied herself with household chores, I would sit on my bedroom floor talking and playing with people who seemed happy to be interacting with me. I never questioned who they were, why they were there, or how they got in. To a child of three and four years old, it didn't matter. The important part of my day was that I had someone to play with. At some point, I revealed my playmates' existence to my mother. This is when I learned the concept of *imaginary*. These people were not real, she said. They were my imagination.

Many children have an imaginary friend or two. For my mother, I suppose, it was easier to grasp than thinking there was something not right with me. After all, we were as normal a family as we could possibly be. We read books. We sang songs. We did arts and crafts. We did not sit and talk to… air. At least, not seriously.

To believe that these *friends* were not real was encompassed in the fear of the disbeliever. Or, maybe, they were believers who were afraid to believe. Being only six years old would have made me a believer because I hadn't had time to learn to disbelieve. I had not yet begun trying to invalidate all I could not understand. Either way, we moved into neighboring East Orange, leaving behind any memory of the people no one could see but me. But moving from one neighborhood to another did not take away my ability to feel energy and quickly assess truth and motivation. I just didn't know what to make of it.

As time moved on, it may have appeared that I was growing into a typical adolescent with typical imperfections and insecurities but I was fitting into fewer social crevices with ease. Like most youngsters, I lived in mortal fear of being viewed as different. Yet, I was more interested in knowing if the supernatural folklore I saw on television and read about in books was real versus playing with dolls, which didn't have the same appeal. There was no intrigue or mystique, nothing to pull together answers about what was beyond where I was. And I never truly grasped that my perspectives were as dissimilar to my immediate environment as was the chemistry of oil to water, as peanut butter looked to jelly, as was Superman's mission compared to Lex Luthor. Unable to put my finger on the pulse of what was going on inside my mind, esthetically, and spiritually, I was out of the loop. Nowhere better or worse. Just, well, *different*.

~ MY THIRD EYE ~

To clarify my limited credentials and humble qualifications to write this book, I am a seer (see-er). That is, I have an ability to visualize, in my mind's eye, certain information, behaviors, and characteristics of others that I would otherwise have no knowledge of, or access to. The information can be received visually or audibly. The visions begin extemporaneously, with little or no provocation. During the course of any day, I can randomly attract someone's life force and a movie (of sorts) will begin to play inside of my mind's eye, for only me to see. Sounds outlandish, doesn't it? Well, I assure you, it's real.

I can view a person in a moment of his or her life, in an environment I have never been. I can feel the sensation of those moments, watching the action as it unfolds. These visions can be of a family member or friend, a new acquaintance or stranger. Attached will be details of an event that has occurred or destiny waiting to happen. It can transpire during the course of a face-to-face dialogue, a telephone conversation, or sensing someone's life force as I interact with a mutual connection. A spiritual link is all that is required.

I may see a descriptive word or succinct phrase. The words are always direct and clear, often accompanied by a prodding to verbalize what has appeared in this ethereal window inside of my mind. There may be a sequence of numbers or specific colors associated with a specific person. And there is always a strong sense of perception pervading these moments. I have seen past trauma or warning of trouble if certain deeds persist. Many times, a spiritual force will nudge me to share these visions. If I choose not to, the same information will appear in my mind's eye until I convey it or dismiss myself from the connection.

Just inside of my head is a voice, the sole source providing the data to this information that, logically, I could not know. Well, for lack of any better interpretation, I have given it the value of a voice, though I am not certain that it is. It narrates the images perusing my mind but no one else can hear it, making it more comparable to a thought. However, it isn't my voice or thoughts in motion. At least, I don't think it is. I am not consciously envisaging any particular person or their life experiences. It just… happens. As I become aware of certain details, a sensation of *knowing* washes over me. Though I rarely understand how it interlocks with the life I am seeing, I already know it to be true.

The knowledge I receive seems to come from nowhere in particular. I am never afraid of it but I am not always assertive in sharing it. Many times, my greater self (the self that is confident and sure) will struggle with my lesser self (the self that prefers to remain oblivious). Often, my dilemma becomes how to begin a conversation and, in just a few minutes, maybe seconds, segue into revealing personal moments with a person I don't know well or not at all.

The Eye of Horus: An ancient Egyptian symbol of protection, power, and good health. Also known as the watchful and all-seeing eye, it is synergetic with the third eye chakra, which governs our intuition, connecting our conscious mind with our subconscious mind.

Seeing is similar to recalling a particular occasion and having it play back across your mind. The modification is that it isn't my reminiscence. Try this: close your eyes. Think about one of your happiest, saddest, or most humorous moments. Resuscitate that emotion. Picture the people involved. Relive the details, the words, the sounds. This is not difficult, is it? It does not matter if you are recalling a recent incident or one that happened years prior. Our experiences remain with us, with no allegiance to time. We may not remember every detail, but they exist nonetheless.

Now, think of your neighbor. Think about when he or she was in grade school, when they got their first job or met the love of their life. Can you calculate the longevity of their marriage, or see their best career path? More than likely you cannot because it is not your experience. It does not exist within the confines of your memory, inside your mind. A seer, however, is able to transcend the boundaries of the mind, connecting on a spiritual level. The information and images then become apparent within the seer's realm of cognizance. It could be visual, audible, an aroma, or a burst of energy, but will manifest in the manner in which that person can connect to the universe and its forces.

... she has a dark complexion and thick legs, not like her mother... before she passes, she has to say what needs to be said... he is there, around a fire contained in a barrel, with others who have nowhere to go... there was no life force; it was as if he didn't exist...

The only difference between what you are able to evoke and what a seer sees is that you are reflecting and the seer is not. That is to say, ordinarily, we can only recollect what we recognize as having occurred. As a personal experience, the information is stored and reviewed at will. Without this point of reference, however, there is no attachment for your brain to refer, as in a memory. However, while I may not share your personal experience from the perspective of personally experiencing it, a link to a spiritual storehouse exists. Here resides all causes, effects, facts, and information. And it can be accessed.

~ A RELUCTANT PSYCHIC ~

While some may be in awe of psychic ability, I acknowledge mine with a touch of whimsy. Sure, it sounds exciting and profoundly mystical but it can be daunting. Apparitions and visions and voices… oh my!

Many people are aware at an early age of being able to predict future events, know of others they have never met and, yes, see the dead. Some embrace their abilities with exuberance and mindfulness and may have had the good fortune to have a supportive environment to develop their skills. Others may choose to keep their psychic ability secret for fear of non-acceptance in our oft-unaccepting society. Then, there are those like me, with intuitive predispositions and no burning desire to be this way.

Psychic ability is a serious responsibility and something I have not always been prepared, or anxious, to accept. It encroaches on my desire to remain anonymous. As I have grown older, though I have become less concerned with outside approval, I still pause at sharing the knowledge I receive. I am still hesitant with a world that may consider me two cents short of a nickel. Truth told, not everyone believes in psychic ability and then, not everyone believes in me.

Clairvoyant / Psychic / Seer / Intuit:
An unusually perceptive person, sensitive to non-physical phenomena; a person with extraordinary spiritual insight.

Having had difficulty accepting my own abilities to communicate with the universe, I often find it challenging to view myself as a guiding light for others, through their trials and tribulations. I shudder at the thought of being the advisor who mistakenly sends someone left instead of right, sinking into oblivion. It can happen. No one is perfect. And not everyone is amenable to having aspects of their life exposed. Particularly to a stranger. After all, no permission had been sought, and none granted, to access these secrets. It's why I stay out of other people's medicine cabinets while in their home. It's an invasion of privacy, of spirit space and, honestly, there are things I simply don't want to know about other people. Therefore, I vacillate at involving myself in the personal affairs of others. But, in an instant, I will get the information and like ticker tape at One Times Square, the images and words go 'round and 'round my mind…

… there is a much younger girl who carries her grandmother's karma… I'm sorry I didn't protect you… these are your golden years… your talent is exceptional but your heart is what takes you there… you can't seem to announce to the world who you are… tsk, it's a double-edged sword… she is soaring… her faith is strong…

I am adjusting to the images that arrive, with no notice, in my mind. I am becoming more comfortable with admitting that I can see dead people, that I can hear their whispers. And I am certainly more certain of their eternal existence. But I find it strange that, while I have access to others' information, I cannot foresee my own future. If I could, what a difference a day would make. But life often provides its own checks and balances and not being able to predict my own tomorrows may be a remedy for remaining mentally sound. Relatively, of course. Imagine knowing what would happen before every turn of the page. There would be no surprises, no special moments of discovery, no quiet time. I knew a psychic who once shared with me that her own energy quickly depletes because she is constantly introduced to other spirits. She almost never rests. And so, I am content with not knowing everything. I will not deliberately concentrate on someone else's life to get the 411. If it's for me to know, the spirits will make it known. Until then, I'm good.

2 WHAT DO YOU BELIEVE?

Housing all that matters, one's belief system creates one's perspective on life and living. The sincerity of our hopes, the intensity of our fears, the depth of our ignorance, or the magnitude of our self-worth are all derived from what we choose to believe or disbelieve. It is through this structure that we venture through life, assessing and assigning value and validity to everything and everyone. But from where do we glean our views and how often do we re-examine our perspectives?

Standards

Standards are limiting by nature and, in essence, only barometers of one person or entity's capacity. Our stance on matters at hand is often set into motion based on another's opinion, interpretation, or (in)ability to comprehend. Captured from birth, we are conditioned into typical ways of viewing the world, learning what is good, what is bad, what is acceptable, what is not. We learn boundaries to be cautious of and lines to dare not cross. From these perspectives we often, and unthinkingly, perpetuate the notion that what does not look like me, act like me, have the same nuances as me, is an outsider, an enemy, the problem. We often create a dividing line between what we have come to view as *normal*, versus all that seems out of that scope.

Standard: typical, ordinary, customary.

What if we were to erase these imaginary dividing lines? What could happen if, instead of sitting contently inside circles of standards, we venture out, creating new ripples, viewing and *re*viewing life from a higher perspective? We may realize there is no atypical, irregular, or abnormal. We may discover there are simply multiple strata of who we are or can be.

~ LIFE ~

How much untapped energy is in the universe? Does it include our legends and myths, ghosts and spirits? Too vast to rationalize, life seems to thrive brilliantly outside of our comprehension of it. Do we really know what is true and what is not? Ancient civilizations were fascinatingly comprised of people with a heightened sense of spirituality. Believing unabashedly in various gods and goddesses, deities and spirits, they sought guidance from these powerful energies, whether waging a battle against other great factions or engaged in struggles within themselves. The forces could be summoned at a moment's notice. Serving and symbolizing diverse purposes and influences, the good forces functioned to assist and protect, while the evil spirits created confusion and chaos. Freely roaming the galaxy, the decision as to which of these spirits manifested rested solely within the heart of the seeker. That was power.

Can we definitively say that these entities did not exist outside the minds of the storytellers? Were they more than parables intended to teach a lesson, or simply animated fables designed to entice the imagination? Perhaps, this was a way of communicating the truth of the expansiveness of our universe. Perhaps, seeing other energies is not as implausible as we may think. We seem to have lost the ability to connect to the cosmos with any great level of awareness. Today, in our daily grind to make ends meet, we live hectic lives that, oftentimes, leave us spiritually deflated.

~ FEAR/RELATIVE SANITY ~

How does fear of the unknown begin? We are all conditioned, to some degree or another, on how to be afraid and what to be afraid of. I grew up in an era that viewed the paranormal as anomalous, illusory, or mysterious. We knew about it but… not really. We didn't believe it… yet, we hid from it, we were afraid. Of ghosts. Of demons. Of dying at the hands of something that no one could coherently explain. Moreover, the more we didn't understand, the more fearful we became.

At four or five years old, my own mother provided me the platform by which to consider the supernatural. From Yokohama, Japan, she was college-educated and an educator herself. Honest and hardworking, she placed high value on rational thinking. With all she believed in, I believed in her. There was one opinion, however, that I found difficult to reconcile. According to the woman I trusted completely, there existed a being named *the devil*. The antithesis of goodness, it was the epitome of evil, able to twist anyone into its slave. And, my mother ever so cautiously informed us, certain behaviors, such as whistling at night, served as incantations, calling it to life. Whoa...

'... let me assert my firm belief that the only thing we have to fear is fear itself — nameless, unreasoning, unjustified terror which paralyzes needed efforts to convert retreat into advance.'
Franklin D. Roosevelt (1933 inaugural address)

I was confused. A preschooler, I hadn't yet developed any religious fortitude. I thought of nothing in a spiritual context. My only reference point to this devil was what I had seen on the TV, this cartoonish character, dressed in a red body suit, with pointed ears and a tail. It was hardly menacing, and all for amusement. Wasn't it? Therefore, though I did not outwardly question the validity of what my mother said, I had my doubts. And now, I felt forced to make a decision. Was it real or was it not?

I was also not so sure if my mother truly believed in what she was saying as much as it was a ploy to get us (mainly my brother) to behave.

However, because of my biological tie and reverent dynamic with my parent, I felt obliged to go along. If my mother thought the devil was real, then, I should also. I became conscious of not whistling, especially at night, and though I did not completely believe or understand, when rainstorms thundered through the courtyard of our project apartment building, my brother's naturally pointed ears caused me consternation. I would shiver at the prospect of there being any *devil* nearby.

My brother, a sci-fi enthusiast, contributed to my views on the underworld by frequently rallying me into watching every horror movie he could find. We saturated our minds with a smorgasbord of surreal characters doing inhuman things. But each time afterwards, he was the one who had difficulty falling asleep. Someone else needed to be awake to distract the ghouls that now prowled his mind. To help himself, he cleverly invented a game of let's-see-who-can-stay-awake-the-longest. There were only two rules: 1) my brother would select the movie we would watch and 2) whichever of us could stay awake the longest was the winner. Yay.

It was also quietly understood that the winner would be alone, subject to being hunted by whatever monster found its way into the room. Not only was this never emphasized, my brother never divulged the fact that I, the little sister, was the sacrifice. Each time, he would will himself to sleep and, figuratively speaking, was dead to the world, untouchable. Creatures didn't care about sleepers. They gravitated towards the runners and the screamers. And that would have been me. I would be the target because I was awake, trying to win this stupid game.

I finally began creating my own illogical fears. For decades, Alfred Hitchcock's classic film *The Birds* had an unimaginable impact on my psyche. A mere child of six, on the rare day that I was late for school, I walked the half-mile alone. Petrified, I hurried along, tightly squinting my eyes so no bird could peck them out. Never afraid of being snatched by a stranger or struck by a car, my panic rested in the imagery of an attack of soaring, screaming vertebrates. *Aaaggghh!* These are the contributors to why I am not your bravest soul when it comes to the paranormal realm.

Spaceships and Aliens

Globally, UFO (Unidentified Flying Object) sightings are not uncommon. In the United States, recorded incidents go back as far as the 1940s, along with news of spaceship landings, human abductions, and government cover-ups. Since one cannot cover up what does not exist, we now know there are unidentified flying objects, as well as foreign identified flying objects. And if we accept the existence of these aircraft (and we have), wouldn't it be reasonable to believe there is also a pilot?

Have beings from other planets infiltrated our society? Are they sitting amongst us, morphing into visually acceptable (human) forms? How do they sustain themselves? This would make them superior beings, dwelling in an unfamiliar atmosphere, without specialized breathing apparatus, learning foreign modes of socialization. Fantastic transformations and logistics would have to be put into motion to enable them to go without detection. Then, what would be their purpose here? For that matter, what is ours?

Ghosts

As far as I knew, ghosts were the souls of dead people, with hideous faces, raspy voices, and questionable intentions. Some of them appeared furled in chains, exemplifying the tortured soul, and some just flitted about, determined to scare the human who was actually paying attention. I knew to avoid them at all costs. But I was also curious. What, exactly, were souls? Did they exist in an alternate reality, another dimension of life? How are we able to see them? At ten years old, I had no real idea and when the opportunity arose to gather more information, I seized it.

In the late 1960s, parents networked to get their offspring jobs as soon as we were old enough. My mother snagged my brother a job helping Mr. Sanders clean a local church. Mr. Sanders was our school crossing guard by day and would moonlight on the weekends doing custodial work. By my estimations, he was *old*. Forty, if he was a day. Of solid character, he was a former military man and now supported my sibling's claim that the church they cleaned was haunted. I had no reason to disbelieve either of them. Actually, I did believe. Moreover, given our childhood, I was impressed that my brother could work in *any* environment he thought was haunted. Therefore, if he had seen a ghost and lived to tell, I had to see it for myself.

Apparition / Ghost / Spirit:
A ghostly figure; the vitality of a dead person; the sentient part of a person.

After repeated begging, my mother finally relented and allowed me to tag along. It was a one-time-only opportunity and I had to first agree to the rules. There were always rules. 1) I had to stay out of the way and, 2) if I were to get scared, I would have to wait it out. No one would be bringing me home. I gladly accepted the terms and excitedly looked forward to seeing my first ghost.

I had seen this church on Park Avenue many times in the daylight. Now, with the darkness of night and dimness of the streetlights, it had a shadowy, ominous look. I had a brief second thought about being there but the deal was sealed and staying outside, alone in the car, was not an option. I went in.

The grey brick structure had the customary stained glass windows and hardwood floors. The room that housed the pews and pulpit was echoic and empty of people. While my brother and Mr. Sanders went about their business of cleaning, I stayed in the kitchen, listening to the whirring sounds of the vacuum and the thumping of garbage cans. *Bo-ring*. After a short while, I reluctantly accepted that there was no ghost. At least, not on this night.

The bumps and knocks did start eventually and I convinced myself they were nothing more than radiators and sewage pipes. However, I could not explain away the organ music, coming from the opposite end of the church. I immediately deduced that if we were all *here*, there was something else *there*. I did not run to investigate. Oh, no. I did not take the opportunity to find out who, or what, had wandered in. Instead, I ran to find my knights in shining armor who, fortunately, were nearby, unconcerned by the sounds. They had heard it before and their cool, calm, and collected demeanor kept me from becoming hysterical.

I now stuck close to my brother and Mr. Sanders. So close, you could not have poured water between us. There was no space. When the time came to go home, I was the first out the door. I was never certain if this was a real event, if a parishioner had been in the church that night, or if it was a joke, played at my expense. I was certain, however, that my ghost-busting days were indefinitely suspended. I was ill prepared to face what I did not understand. What, exactly, was this energy?

~ ENERGY ~

Energy can become evident in a variety of ways, positive or negative. It can manifest through a physical source or remain only sensations of occupied space; something we can feel but cannot see or touch. I am not an expert on this topic and everything you read here is only my effort to further understand it as it relates to spirit.

Energy is non-physical and is not gender specific. Until it manifests in a physical container, i.e., a jar, a body, a tree, it is an unseen force. Descriptions of male or female, tall or short, black, white, brown, or yellow, exists only to help the human further identify things in existence. The universe doesn't seem to have need for such information. How then, are we able to differentiate between our relatives and friends after they have transitioned from life to death (as we know it), and then reappear in spirit form? How do we know who's who? And why are there *hauntings*?

I don't have all of the answers but I do know that spirits often reveal a characteristic that would describe them as we knew them in a physical life. They were humorous, they were stern, they liked a certain color... this serves as confirmation of their presence. Spirits attach to certain people and return to physical environments to which they are familiar. It's interesting but, no, I don't know *why* or *how* this happens. If I knew, this book would be a different narration. Maybe, possibly, the simple answer is that these encounters are meetings of energy.

Have you ever felt you were not alone, though there was no one else around? In my mid-teens, I was an avid reader and books were a primary source of information for me. Unlike conversation, no topic was off-limits and it seemed harmless to borrow a book from the local library about the occult. I was curious. Let it stand that I was not interested in becoming an occultist. I only wondered about the purpose and fundamental beliefs of the group. While the title of the book escapes me now, and I don't remember if it was fact or fiction, I do remember my experience.

Alone that evening, I settled onto the sofa in the living room with my reading material. I was captivated with this information of clandestine nighttime meetings and sacrificial rituals. Soon, I felt a distinct shift in the atmosphere. It began to feel oddly dense and portentous. Startled, I was certain I was sharing my space with something I could not see. Associating this change with the book I was reading, I immediately closed it. I wanted no interaction with any negative entity. To counteract my fear, I shifted to happy thoughts… *la, la, la, la, la, la…* and felt the energy evaporate.

I never finished reading the book, returning it to the library as soon as humanly possible. Never interested in invocations, potions, or evil spirits, I had no intention of getting involved with this. I have never read another book on the occult. In fairness, I have no real information on occultism and this is not an effort to minimize or demonize it.

It is only my experience. My conclusion may not be your conclusion.

Around this time, I helped family friends move into their new condominium. It was summer and I stayed the night in the bare guestroom, making a bed on the newly carpeted floor. The electricity was not on yet and only the moon, through the curtainless window, provided light. Sounds of the natural environment filtered through the darkness, a vast difference from the constant purr of city life in East Orange. After comfortably drifting off to sleep, I opened my eyes to the disturbing feeling that I was not alone. Lying on my stomach, I had a deep sense of vulnerability at my back, as though someone was there. Staying as still as I could, I listened intently for any sounds of movement. There was none. As casually as I could, I turned over to get a clearer view of the room. Through slits in my eyes, I could see there was nothing there. The room was as bare as when I had entered. But if no one else is here, what am I feeling?

Taking a deep breath, I made a leap for the door, hoping nothing would reel me back in. Sprinting into the hall, I stopped short. The rest of the house was dark and still. With nothing behind me, I couldn't go running and screaming into the night, disturbing everyone. How would that look for a Jersey Girl? I had to compose myself. I had to think about how I was going to wait out the night.

Positioning myself in the doorway with the lower half of my body in the guestroom and the upper half in the hall, whatever was here would have to drag me either way. That would give me a fighting chance from whatever was lurking about. The sun could not rise soon enough. I stayed awake as long as I could before succumbing to sleep.

I woke to the warm rays of the sun floating graciously through the windows, making the previous night seem like a hallucination. Troubles always seem worse at night, don't they? And there I was, waking up in the middle of the doorway, feeling a bit foolish. At the breakfast table, I shared my mid-night activity, hoping someone would say they had had the exact same experience. It didn't happen. Non-believers in spiritual phenomena, no one believed in ghosts. They had, however, walked past me as I lay sleeping in the middle of that doorway…

~ DREAMS ~

We all have dreams, whether we remember them or not. There are colors and outlines, people and places. Some we know, most we don't. What are these images based upon?

> *Who are these folks and why are they communing in my mind?*

In a dream state, we can experience an array of emotions tied to people we know, places we have been, or circumstances we have lived. We can dream of people we do not recognize or find ourselves wandering through unknown geographical territories, running from who-knows-what. We may have recurring dreams of nightmarish conditions or open our eyes to find ourselves smiling broadly. Is there any rhyme or reason?

When asleep, are we conscious of our thoughts or behavior? Some theorists suggest that dreams are not only a recounting of events but also contain subconscious desires or fears. Anxiety from daily stresses could manifest during these unrestrained moments. When I worked in law enforcement, I would occasionally dream of being involved in a shootout with a malfunctioning weapon. Rather than working as projectiles, the bullets would just drop from my gun, making me unable to return fire. This was, most likely, a subconscious manifestation of knowing the dangers of my job.

Studies have given us information on several stages of sleep but have no absolute conclusions as to *how* or *why* they occur. We begin our course between being awake and drifting off to sleep. We become listless, slowly losing muscle tone and our ability to react physically. If we are holding onto anything, it drops. Our hearing diminishes, our breathing slows, and our heart rate and body temperature will change. We slowly float away from our world of lively activity. Now dreaming, we may become daring. We may be frightened. We may be confused. We can include ourselves in scenarios we would not normally, or deliberately, put ourselves in while awake.

Stages of a dream:
- Drowsiness
- Light sleep
- NREM (Non-Rapid Eye Movement)
- REM (Rapid Eye Movement)

Our deepest sleep occurs during the NREM stage where we are less cognizant of our environment. Physically, we can toss and turn but we cannot consciously respond to whatever is going on around us. Our brainwaves are slow moving and sleepwalking will likely occur here, in the transition back into wakefulness. During the

REM part of the cycle, our brain will begin waking, though our body remains at rest. Our eyes begin to move rapidly and our breathing picks up pace. Most of our dreaming occurs at this stage.

Can dreams be a presentiment, a premonition? Is there information contained in these minutes of slumber that coincide with actual events and times? Renowned prophet Edgar Cayce had the ability to predict the future via his visions, delivered while in a sleep state. Some of his documented dreams/premonitions rang true over a period of years, even after his death in 1945. Where does information of future events exist in the mind? And, does every dream have substance?

Though dreams are not my psychic forte, it is one of my earliest psychic experiences. In 1972, in my mid-teens, my brother had proudly enlisted in a branch of the U.S. military. He was blissful and I was ecstatic. Having established himself the ruler of everything in our home not nailed down, all I could recognize was freedom from his older sibling reign. No more made up rules that applied to no one but me. It meant he would be away in training for months. It was a win/win situation.

A couple of weeks had passed since my brother had left for boot camp and everything was good. Enjoying the pretense of being an only child, I woke one morning with remnants in my mind of seeing my brother standing outside our front door, waiting for someone to open it. There was a faint remembrance of a knocking at the door and I got up to answer it. There was no one there. It was strange. My brother wasn't due to return home but I had a feeling. He was coming home.

Cognitive: perceptive or aware.
Precognitive: the ability to foresee future events.

Later, serious in revealing this information to my mother, I expected her to be equally serious in receiving it. Her raised eyebrow and brusque, *"Oh?"* told me otherwise. She did not believe me. Who could blame her? I had no proof. It was my dream against the backdrop of the United States of America's military force. Not only did they have the agenda, they created the agenda. They had the questions and the answers. Most of all, my mother was not versed in psychic ability and did not believe anyone could predict the future. Particularly, her daughter.

A day or so later, I answered a knock at the door. Released on a technicality, there stood my brother, his duffle bag slung over his shoulder, and my vindication on his back. My savior. Despite his disappointment at being home, I was glad. He made my life worthy again. Getting along as though old friends reunited, I listened intently to the details of my brother's return and I looked at everything he wanted to share with me. Especially interesting was a stream of black and white photos he had taken at the airport, in one of those small, phone booth-like containers. I looked at these new pictures and noticed that the jacket my brother had on was not the dark wool Navy pea coat he was now wearing. Then, neither of these coats was what he had worn when he had left for training.

As I looked at these photos of my brother wearing clothes I had never seen, I saw a hint of color. A mental image of the word *purple* appeared. The jacket was purple. I was confident about this information and asked my brother. He said yes, it was, and wondered how I knew this. Not knowing how to explain it, I shrugged it off, saying it *looked purple*. Whether or not it was a satisfactory answer, it was accepted.

My brother explained that at his discharge, the military no longer had his personal belongings. In compensation, he received attire from someone else's induction. I smiled. A stylish dresser, I knew my brother would have preferred his own full-length leather coat. This nylon bubble jacket in the photograph was no reflection of his taste in clothes.

The Navy pea coat my brother wore home came into his possession at the airport. He had met a would-be seafarer, discharged and disenchanted. Wanting to sever all ties with the U.S. military, including his clothing, he offered a trade. Here, these two men, strangers in the midst of the sagas of their lives, swapped coats. There was no way I could have known. The conclusion was that the man walked away with the bubble jacket, my brother had his coveted pea coat, and I received my absolution. But questions lingered. How did I know my brother was returning home and how did I know the color of that jacket?

The Lucas Home

We have known the Lucas family for more than half a century. They lived in Newark, New Jersey in a large Victorian style home, replete with high ceilings, hardwood floors, and a wraparound porch I love to this day. I never spent an enormous amount of time there but it was a familiar and safe space. The years passed quickly and everyone took flight in different directions of personal growth. Though our communication was infrequent, the spirit of friendship remained consistent.

In my mid-30s, for no particular reason, I started having an occasional dream of being in the Lucas home. In the very last one, I had gone to visit. I found the inside covered in soot, obviously due to a fire. The dream was not a long detailed one. There were no people involved and no one was home. I woke not knowing how to interpret this information. I didn't know if it was an event that had already occurred or a premonition. And I wasn't certain that it wasn't *just a dream*.

I shared this with my mother and asked that she make a care call, which she did immediately. Reportedly, the house had been sold and though there were no specifics, it had caught fire. Fortunately, no one was in the home. More than twenty years later, I have not had another dream about that house. I don't know the significance of this dream. I only know that I had it.

~ WHISPERS IN THE DARK ~

In 1977, having to decide what I should be doing with the rest of my life, I enrolled at the New

Brunswick campus of Rutgers University. The co-ed dormitories at Livingston College had a functioning underground tunnel linking them and it was always abuzz with young life, going from one place to another. On the weekends, most students left the campus, heading home or elsewhere. With the exception of a blizzard, my roommate spent her weekends in Trenton while I stayed behind, basking in the solitude of having my own space, even if only for a couple of days. The rooms had a large picture window and through mine, I had a view of center court. I could catch a glimpse of the peace and quiet evolving as everyone left the grounds, one by one, as all signs of life slowed to a minimum.

My room was on the first floor, facing an entrance/exit door. During the week, there was always noise of it opening and shutting, as someone came and went. On the weekends, it stood still. On this specific Saturday morning, the buildings were quiet and nearly deserted. By evening, with just a handful of students left from the mass exodus, I took notice of the calm. There were no sounds of conversations to overhear. No busy-ness of this or that. It was peaceful. After showering in the communal bathroom out in the corridor, I started the short walk back to my room. I was thinking of nothing in particular. Half-way to my destination, behind me in the empty hall, someone called my name. Well, it wasn't just anyone. It was Chieko, a longtime family friend. A friend who had recently passed away.

I had known Chieko for, at least, a dozen of my nineteen years. I had last seen her during the summer, at a large picnic gathering. She was ill, but she was laughing and smiling, determined to enjoy every moment she had left. She made her transition soon afterwards. Not wanting to think about death and dying, I did not attend her funeral. Now, she was here.

Chieko's voice, in life, was not the demure one expected of Japanese women. It was commanding and unmistakable. She spoke English with a noticeable Japanese accent and attached the word *chan* to the names of all younger people she knew (Mary-*chan*, Billy-*chan*, etc.). In the Japanese language, this was a term of endearment and affection, normally extended from an adult to a child. My mother's age, Chieko always attached this moniker to my name. It didn't matter how old I had become. Now, on this day, there was no mistaking her distinctive voice, her undeniable accent. It was the only name she ever called me and it was what she called me now…

At this precise instance, I was unsure about where I was. I was certain however, that time was standing still. Hesitating in mid-step, I felt as though I was living out one of those horror movies I had watched as a child, the one where the getaway was in painful slow motion. I didn't turn around to see who, or what, was there. Actually, I couldn't turn around. I was frozen, terrified that any acknowledgement of whatever I had heard would cause it to spring further to life, right in front of me. Oh, I was scared.

I looked straight ahead and ordered myself to continue walking. I had to get out of the hall. Without looking back, with an exact quickness, I rushed to my room, opened the door, and jumped inside. I prayed that the thick, solid door would shut out whatever was on the other side. At least, I hoped it was on the other side. I was not certain how ghosts traveled and hadn't thought seriously about it for many years. I had decided I didn't really want to know and pushed away any thoughts of it, tucking them at the back of my mind, leaving them there, indefinitely. Now, I wondered. Did they really migrate through walls and doors, and seep through cracks and crevices? I watched and I waited. Was I safe?

If life is energy and death is an absence of that energy, but if, in fact, energy never dies, what then, is death?

This could not have been a prank. First, most people had already vacated the premises. Even with the few left, who else here knew Chieko? And if they knew her, how could they have mimicked her voice so perfectly? I could not make any sense of it. I knew that Chieko had died. What I did not know was how I had heard her call my name.

Unable to rationalize it, there was no way I was staying on campus. I was not going to risk seeing Chieko in the middle of the night, especially while I was alone. I strategized: the campus bus could get me to the train station in town. I could ride the rail into Newark and catch a city bus up Central Avenue to my mother's apartment in Orange. At minimum, it was a two-hour trip and a great plan, however, the campus bus operated on a sparse schedule on weekends and had already stopped running for the night. Serious about getting out, I pooled my limited resources and, like a thief in the night, I was gone.

I returned to school on Monday, repaid all debts related to my trip home, and never said a word to anyone. Who would believe me? From then on, I went home every weekend. No one could have paid me to stay.

Leaving the dorms of Livingston College on the weekends did not discourage the spirits from finding me. Simultaneous to my move onto the Rutgers campus, my mother had moved into a quaint, well maintained, three-story apartment building in Orange, New Jersey. Occupied by middle-aged to elderly people, it was beyond quiet. The slightest noise in the halls would reverberate down the linoleum-covered floors, cutting the silence, wafting under every door. As a security measure, there was a speaker system at the main entrance, allowing residents to identify visitors before permitting them onto the premises. I felt comfortably safe there. This, however, was a temporary situation.

Now home on the weekends, I did as young people would do, burning the midnight oil with marathon telephone conversations with Debbie, a college friend. We paralleled in a nerdy kind of way though, at that time, I would not have described myself (or her) as such. Her sister had married one of my brother's best friends. We were practically family-in-law. We could talk about everything and anything into the wee hours of the morning, cooking up home fries in our respective kitchens. After one of our chats, I was lying on the sofa in my mother's living room, attempting to get in a few hours of sleep before the sun rose. With everything still, I heard chattering outside in the hall. Though muffled, I could clearly hear voices engaged in dialogue. Low and whispery, I assumed these were people going into one of the other apartments. After several minutes, however, I could still hear them. And it seemed that now, whoever was out there, had moved directly in front of my mother's front door.

I was alarmed. Loitering around anyone's door went against apartment-living etiquette. It was an unwritten rule, but every apartment dweller knew this was an encroachment of personal space. I assumed there was more than one person because I heard what seemed to be a give-and-take conversation. What were they doing at my mother's door?

My being delusional never crossed my mind. I was very sane. I was not involved with alcohol or drugs and knew this was not in my head. Those voices were real. To get a glimpse, I slowly made my way to the door, careful to step just right, to avoid the squeaks in the floorboards. Looking out of the peephole, I could not see anyone but I could definitely hear the voices.

To say that I was concerned and unnerved would be an understatement. My entire body was on red-hot alert. Whoever was out there might be hiding on either side of the door, conspiring to break into the apartment. The kitchen was next to the front door and I slid in and armed myself with two steak knives. Stationed like a ninja, I watched the doorknob intently for signs of tampering. I waited. And I waited. There was no movement.

The voices eventually went away, leaving me relieved but uneasy. I had no understanding as to what had occurred. With little information, my first thought was not *paranormal occurrence*. Not at all. I did not make the connection between this and hearing Chieko's voice. And I did not connect the dots with my imaginary friends from childhood. Actually, I had forgotten all about them. And now, I was going to forget about this. Or, at least, I would try.

Weeks later, with Chieko's voice still ringing in my ears, I confided in my mother. I withheld telling her about hearing the voices in the hall. It seemed too bizarre and I couldn't explain it. Though there was no extended dialogue, unlike years prior, when I predicted my brother's return, she did not look at me as though I had lost my mind. This time, she accepted my words. Perhaps, she had also gotten a visit.

During this time, my brother shared one of his own ghostly experiences with me. He was good friends with a family in Plainfield, New Jersey and was given free access to their home. In the wee hours of this one morning, he arrived after a night out. Letting himself in, he went up the stairs and passed an unfamiliar man on the landing. Thinking this was a guest of someone in the house, my brother extended a simple greeting to the man, who did not respond. My brother continued up the stairs and retired for the night. Later, he mentioned seeing this man to the family. Some were familiar with him. They said he was not an invited guest. They said he was *a ghost*.

Even a move across state lines did not keep the spirits at bay. In 1987, working the mid-shift as a police officer, I would return home after midnight. You could have easily heard a pin drop on our tarred street. I had moved from the north to the south for a less loud environment and this was heaven. Though I did not like the bullfrogs sitting on my walkway, I could stop and breathe in the fresh night air. I could watch the swaying trees and glistening moon without concern of being accosted by robbers. In the morning, cardinals and blue jays would perch on our porch, singing us awake, and rabbits and chipmunks would scurry about. It was easy getting lost in the peace. However, now inside my home, interrupting the silence, were voices outside my carport door.

Immediately thinking *perpetrator* I turned off the lights and positioned myself at the door. Peeking out of the small windowpane, I could not see anyone. But I definitely heard the voices. Not wanting to walk into an ambush, I waited inside. Weapon ready, I watched the door for the first sign of movement. I made no connections with this current experience and anything previous. I should have, but I didn't. I was mentally and spiritually far-removed from the spirit world. After seconds that seemed like many minutes, the voices faded and whoever was outside was gone.

I continued to disengage from any thought of the supernatural, preferring to believe someone had been on my property. That was the practical choice. I heard the voices on a few other occasions and on one of these nights my mother saw me frozen at the door, gun in hand. Questioning my sanity, she asked if I was all right. I was fine, I said. Wasn't I? In retrospect, I probably did look rather peculiar standing there, listening to something only I could hear.

I have recently reconnected with Debbie and learned she is clairvoyant. Who knew? Always enjoying open dialogue, we never once conferred about psychic ability. You may be surprised to one day learn that there is more to Uncle George, Cousin Marguerite, or Raymond the Butcher than you would ever guess.

~ PROTECTIVE FORCES ~

Have you ever had an unseen force intervene on your behalf, just before disaster struck? Maybe you were able to identify the spirit of a deceased relative who came to you in a dream, or a friend giving advice to be cautious on a particular day or about a particular person. What are these energies and where is this information from?

Since childhood, with no cause apparent, I feared dying in a car wreck. In any vehicle, I would silently panic, nervous about perishing. It wasn't a result of any experiences in this current lifetime. I had never been in, nor witnessed, any vehicle accident. In fact, we didn't even have a family car. Affecting me into adulthood, I had staved off acquiring a driver's license until I was almost thirty, when I had to consider a more independent mode of transportation. It was a major step in becoming a certified police officer a couple of years later, where driving was a vital part of the job. But I was unable to free myself of my anxiety. By 2001, I had become so distracted by this phobia that I began avoiding highway traffic. I used local streets and back roads whenever possible. If I had to utilize the highway, I would never drive in the fast lane. If I did, it would only be for a short period of time. It was all scripted. Except for this one day...

Saturday, July 20, 2002

Fate. For no particular reason, and unusual for my personality, I abandoned my schedule for the morning, making one spontaneous change after another. Carrying my driver's license had become part of my daily routine and I never left home without it. It was on my mental check-off list. This day, however, I found myself driving home to retrieve it. One thing led to another thing and I was in the fast lane on the interstate. It was early in the day, traffic was not heavy, and I didn't anticipate any problems. Though it seemed to last a lifetime, it all happened very quickly.

The vehicle in front of me swerved into another lane and I was left facing the blinking tail lights of a stalled vehicle. A taxi. To avoid colliding with the other vehicles, I passed into the emergency lane, grazing the concrete divider. I began to fishtail, snaking down the highway. I can still recall the screeching sounds of applying my brakes, trying to halt the inevitable. It seemed that my lifetime concern over being killed in a car crash was becoming a reality.

I heard the words *let it go*, as I countered my car's every movement. It was a confident command

and I realized my car could turn over if I didn't. Relaxing, not knowing what was going to happen, I took my foot off of the brake pedal. I relinquished control of my vehicle. Keeping my hands lightly on the steering wheel, I watched as my car performed maneuvers that seemed to defy gravity. It went in one direction and then another.

I approached the concrete median wall head-on and thought of being crushed from the impact, cut by the broken windshield. I braced myself. I struck the wall and bounced backwards, southward across eastbound lanes. I remember thinking about not wanting to cause a massive accident and not wanting anyone else to be hurt. At this moment, I watched my front bumper begin to peel off of my car, from right to left. There was nothing pulling it. It was just detaching.

I felt as though I was in a time warp. There seemed ample time to think but, in fact, it was all happening in a matter of seconds. My direction of travel had changed again and the momentum sent me sliding sideways, back towards the wall. Facing the opposite direction now, westbound on the eastbound side, I braced for impact with oncoming traffic. Fortunately, there were no other cars, and my vehicle abruptly stopped in the unoccupied HOV lane. And the front bumper just dropped off the car. A police officer arrived and I watched in disbelief as he commandeered the disabled taxi across the highway, to the waiting driver. This vehicle was now drivable.

My sons came to the scene and escorted me to the local hospital for x-rays. There, I recounted this event for them. My youngest son's conclusion was that, on this morning, I had gone to meet my destiny. It was a profound deduction. And then he asked me an odd question. *Who is Papa Cool?*

My grandmother's second husband was better known as Papa Coo. I can only guess the nickname was from his love of singing the blues. Since my grandmother's funeral in 1969, I had seen him only once, soon after she passed. My children were born much later and Papa Coo was not part of any conversations with them. Through the years, news in the family was that he had died but no one knew when, where, or how. With no reference point, I asked my son what made him mention my grandfather. His answer was that he had seen him at my accident site. He said he helped me, turning my car around, preventing me from having a fatal accident.

I believed my son. There was no other reason he would have thought to mention my grandfather. Especially when he was unfamiliar with him. A day or so later, I went to retrieve items from my vehicle at the impound yard. Expecting to see only a vestige of my car, with the exception of minimal front end damage, it was whole. There was no broken glass. All windshields, windows, and mirrors were intact.

I believe a force appeared that day to help change the course of my life. Rest in peace Papa Coo.

We all have segments of life that we accept or deny. We also reserve the right to renegotiate our thoughts and decisions, drawing alternate conclusions, based upon new knowledge or proof. And whether we believe in any religious, secular, philosophical, scientific, or spiritual law or concept is, really, of no consequence to what *is*. A fact cannot be modified because of disbelief or lack of understanding. At some moment, we will have to set aside habituations gained from family, friends and community and examine how we fundamentally view the universal systems. Not only will we have to determine the level of responsibility we will accept for our own being, we will have to determine what it is that we truly believe.

3 PSYCH-ISM 101

For sure, there are cynics of paranormal occurrences and psychic abilities. Without a direct connect or some kind of spiritual base, this phenomenon is sometimes difficult to appreciate or too fantastic to even consider. Compelled to disprove the incredible, the mantra of the non-believer is, *'This is not real. This is an illusion.'* But… is it?

Our five sense organs (eyes, ears, nose, tongue, and skin) discern basic information of sight, hearing, smell, taste, and touch. Ordinarily, we can see and hear up to a certain distance away. We can detect and distinguish various aromas, enjoy tasting a variety of herbs and spices, and feel the difference in temperature of our changing seasons. The sixth sense is our intuition, and goes a step beyond. It is a recognition of spiritual phenomena. It allows us to know life from a more in-depth realm, sensing what is not so obvious.

*Metaphysics / Supernatural / Paranormal:
part of a thought-process that recognizes what is beyond the average sense of perception; an order of existence beyond what is visible; what is not scientifically explainable.*

Years ago, Maya, a friend of my son, had come to visit. As we talked, images began to freely flow through my mind. There was a young man in her home. He walked from the kitchen, into the living room, to the bottom of the stairs. Starting up, he stopped between the fourth and sixth steps, never going completely up.

Maya recounted her recurring dream of a man forcibly entering her home from the back door, at the kitchen. Walking into the living room, to the stairs, he starts up, but never goes beyond the fourth step. We both received, in different ways, the same information. Was it real?

~ DIMENSIONS ~

The universe is multi-layered, or multi-dimension. The three most commonly known dimensions are length, width, and depth. Everything we consider legitimate (our reality) will fit into some form of these measurements. We can measure anything that occupies any area of space. By adding one measurement (dimension) to another, we create a broader, deeper view of the object before us, from the first dimension, to the second dimension, and so forth. The third dimension, or 3D, provides a more comprehensive visual picture than 1D, which is flat and limited.

Our view in the third dimension can always be reformed, giving another viewpoint or perspective, as we move within the parameters of that space. The dimension itself doesn't change but, certainly, our view does. For instance, years ago, the vehicle I was driving was broken into. I realized this later that evening when I could not find my briefcase. I went back and forth in my mind, tracing my steps for the day, attempting to determine the moment of loss. Searching the vehicle, I could find no forced entry. I knew there was something I was not seeing. I took a step back, literally. Crouching, I began another visual sweep, from another angle. There it was. A barely visible puncture to the driver's door, just at the handle, was the point of entry. Changing my vantage point changed the area of observation. I now had a wider range of view of the condition of the vehicle. Now, I could see.

The fourth dimension is time, and the fifth and sixth dimensions are where we begin the possibility of the existence of other worlds. This is where we would find the paranormal. Some believe there are as many as ten or eleven dimensions, of which I am ill-equipped to discuss. There is so much more information available on this topic than I could ever translate here.

Through the generations, the media has provided small doses of information so that we might be able to understand, and visualize, aspects of life from a diverse perspective. From 1959 until 1964 the American public enjoyed one of the most insightful and prolific television series to date, *The Twilight Zone*. Spanning the scope of a magnificent imagination, or so we thought, it was revolutionary. Its anecdotes of life and existence in other spatial realities continue to be relevant.

"There is a fifth dimension, beyond that which is known to man. It is a dimension as vast as space and as timeless as infinity. It is the middle ground between light and shadow, between science and superstition, and it lies between the pit of man's fears and the summit of his knowledge." ~ Rod Serling

This cosmic arena is an extension of our awareness. Often, the only evidence of the existence of this realm is within the spirit of the person experiencing it. As we become more cognizant of time and space, we can better appreciate the enormity of all life, wherever and however, it may manifest. We are not always able to recognize these existences, however, because of self-induced constraints. Many times we see what we choose to see, not what truly exists.

~ TIME and SPACE TRAVEL ~

How does a person travel through time and space? Astral Projection is the assimilation of one's life force into the universal sphere. Since there is an elimination of physical restrictions, there are no limitations to spirit travel. Therefore, spiritually, we could be anywhere, at any time. It is a matter of being conscious of the opportunities we have concerning life in its completeness. It is about manifesting one's own power, connecting with the universe on its most fundamental level, making everything possible.

Saturday, June 3, 2000

In my practice of Nichiren Buddhism, Mr. Yamamoto serves as mentor for living life with integrity, compassion and truth. Though continents apart, I had an opportunity to experience the breadth of his transcendent spirit.

Mr. Yamamoto had built a multi-acre facility in the southern region of the United States, designed for Buddhist members to convene and rejuvenate their faith. The study conferences are weekend-long and filled with learning, prayer, and camaraderie. When I have attended, I have always been spiritually uplifted, bursting with revelations and personal resolutions. After one particular visit, I agreed to share my experience with the membership. Nervous about my presentation, I worried that I would not be able to express what was flowing through my heart in a way that others could understand. Applying my prayers to overcoming these concerns, in an instant, the room went completely dark.

Though I could not see a thing, I could hear the melodic sound of everyone in the room chanting in unison: *nam myoho renge kyo, nam myoho renge kyo, nam myoho renge kyo* (yes, Tina Turner's chant in her biopic, What's Love Got to Do With It). Mr. Yamamoto walked from the back of the room and stopped where I was sitting. To my knowledge, on this day he was not physically in the United States. Yet, now, he was close enough that I could see his red tie, dark jacket, and the waffled texture of his yellow vest. The words *don't worry* emanated from him as he passed me and continued on to the front of the room. In an unwavering voice, he led us in prayer. I felt my own spirit leave my body and sit beside him. The feeling of embracing him as my life mentor was overwhelming.

In the next instant, the room was in its original state. The lights were on and everyone was as they were. There was no indication that anyone else was aware of this episode. There was also no doubt that Mr. Yamamoto had spiritually traveled the globe in response to my prayer, to encourage and reassure me. Afterwards, I consulted with someone who had been in Mr. Yamamoto and his wife's presence several times. Mrs. Edwards acknowledged that the words I had heard, *don't worry*, would have been something he would have said.

~ OUT-OF-BODY EXPERIENCE ~

What causes an out-of-body experience (OBE)? Parapsychology is the study of the paranormal and views an out-of-body experience, also referred to as soul traveling, spirit walking, or astral projecting, as the spiritual aspect detaching from the physical aspect. I experienced this for the first time on November 12, 2003.

I had gone to bed early in the evening and woke up hours later to a feeling of other energy around me. It must have been about ten o'clock by now and my room was completely dark, darker than usual. I knew where I was, but there was something different about this space, at this moment. I had to leave. Feeling groggy, I rose from my bed and stumbled to the door. There was someone on the other side and I had to get their attention.

Transmitting coherent instructions to my hands was difficult. I could not get them to grab the doorknob, to turn it. I tried, but my mind and my body were not in harmony. They were not working together. While I couldn't turn the knob, strangely, I could bang on the door. Or so I thought.

With the palms of my hands, with what seemed like all the power I could muster, I hit the door.

Once, twice, three times. It wasn't forceful enough. My attempts to scream out were laborious and unsuccessful. Tongue-tied, they came out as sounds. Grunts. It seemed I was in a different world, moving in slower motion. My dexterity was gone. I could think it but I could not execute it.

Disoriented, since I could not open the door, I went to lay back down on my bed. I could see the door was slightly ajar and the hall light was on. Someone was definitely there. Anxious to free myself from this lethargy, as quickly as I could manage, I got up again. I walked to the door, striding out of my inertia.

My son was standing there, on the other side of the door, looking smugly into a mirror hanging on the wall. He smiled and greeted me but I was perturbed. In a confrontational tone (I'm sure), I asked why he didn't help me. Well, he said he had heard my voice but I had sounded *weird* and he thought I was kidding. Now, from the look on my face, he knew this was not a joke. I asked if he had heard me banging on the door. No. He did not. However, he did say that when he had heard my voice, he looked into my room. Thinking about it now, he realized it was so dark he could not see a thing. This was unusual because the light from the hall always filtered into my room, illuminating it. This time, it didn't.

My son pointed out that if I had banged on the door, it would have shut. But it didn't. It was ajar. It was all very puzzling. Later, researching this incident, I read that in the spiritual dimension spirits cannot speak. At least, not in the sense of human dialogue. They can only make sounds, which would account for the muffled, moaning sounds I was making. I had entered a spiritual dimension. Why, and how, this happened is baffling. I am certain, however, that it happened.

~ THE MIND vs THE BRAIN ~

Is psychic ability a function of the brain, a matter of intellect, or the condition of a spiritual life? At what point is a person's mental, emotional, or psychic astuteness determined? We know that the brain is a tangible and delicate organ and that any jarring could send it spiraling into a strange mental orbit. The mind, though, is intangible, existing on a non-physical level. How do we gauge its content?

Neuroscience is dedicated to studying the functions of the brain and explores why it reacts/responds as it does. With modern medicine and technology, doctors can diagnose symptoms of erratic behavior, prescribe medications to quell psychosis, or propose psychological therapy. What if these symptoms are not, in fact, part of any illness? What if this is a mind that perceives more than the doctor can imagine?

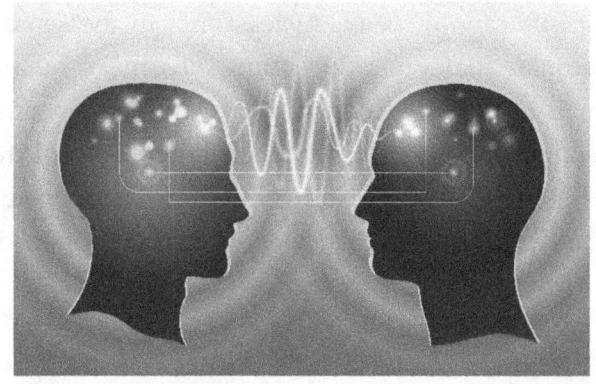

Though we continue to devote great time and effort medically and scientifically to resolving questions regarding the workings of our brain, much of it remains speculative. No one knows completely why the brain functions the way it does. Sigmund Freud and Carl Jung were two prominent psychologists who dedicated much of their lives to examining the brain, the mind, and their distinct purposes and functions. While many of Freud's enquiries and conclusions regarding the human psyche were controversial, he provided a foundation to begin thinking about the conscious and unconscious mind. He held that the unconscious mind holds more information than we suspect. Jung agreed, further articulating that our subconscious mind is the storage space of all idle information. It is our complete memory bank. Even when we do not consciously remember any one thing, it subsists.

By definition, one may assume that the conscious mind is active and the unconscious, inactive. The doctors, however, surmised that both capacities are active, one simply appearing more cognizant. Other famed clinicians have documented their extensive research and personal experience into the metaphysical world, including their conclusions on the subconscious mind. The general assessment is that both consciousnesses are active functions of the brain, housing memories and holding a mass quantity of information. Including that of previous lifetimes. If you believe in such.

~ LIFE *after* DEATH ~

When the human body undergoes the transition to physical non-existence, where goes our intrinsic motivation? What becomes of the source that allowed us the inspiration to love, to laugh, to forgive, to breathe? Do we live only once, with our lives extinguished into nothingness at death? Or will our life experience transfer to another physical form, continuing missions already begun? While some believe death to be a finality, others believe there is a continuation of imperceptible energy. What do you think?

Brian L. Weiss, author (*Many Lives, Many Masters*) and M.D. with a lucrative career in psychiatry, had not given much thought to these questions. Until, that is, he encountered a woman (a nurse, working in the same hospital) suffering with perplexing fears that had created a depressive state of life. Her supervisor recommended Dr. Weiss for a cure.

During routine therapy sessions, the woman could not provide any basis for her emotional breakdown. There was no abuse, neglect, or other trauma. Dr. Weiss furthered his treatment with supervised hypnosis and watched as his patient passed into a subconscious state, then provided information regarding her past lives. The doctor was astounded. He recorded these sessions and included his wife (also a doctor) to bear witness.

The patient began to exhibit a high level of cognizance, revealing specifics even in the lives of the doctor's own family members, whom she had never met. She told of a private tragedy, the heart-breaking death of an infant. She was not privy to the doctor's personal life and she could not have gathered this information through any general conversation. Yet, somehow, this patient knew the details.

*If intuition is inherent information,
what is the origination?*

This experience was, indeed, therapeutic for the patient. It allowed her an opportunity to resolve current quandaries by understanding the root cause. It also provided the doctor an opportunity to explore and understand a broader continuum of life. Unbelievable? Maybe. With *karma* now a plausible concept, suppose we do arrive into our existence with an accumulation of knowledge, of causes and effects, spanning previous lifetimes. Realizing other existences might explain the child prodigy, who is able to comprehend much more than his handful of years would expect. As we accomplish seemingly difficult tasks with ease, it may be an explanation for our natural abilities and inclinations, our scholastic, athletic, and creative flow. It can also exemplify how the altruistic person can meet with misfortune, the selfish gain wealth, and provide illumination of the knowing some of us experience without benefit (seemingly) of a specific lesson.

These could be results of causes made within some other period of life.

~ THE PSYCHIC NETWORK ~

Spanning centuries, societies across the globe have undergone various stages of fascination and fear into this world of healers and sorcerers, shamans and clairvoyants. This ability to know more than anyone was expected to know had been looked upon as something evil and sinister and outside of ordinary townsfolks' ability to comprehend. Fourteenth and fifteenth century Europe expelled thousands of people, putting them to death, in the name of abolishing this thing they called witchcraft. They called the practitioners *witches*.

In 1692, anxiety ignited in colonial Massachusetts as suspicion of the existence of people with the skill to *foresee* spread. The debacle known as the Salem Witch Trials took hold when a group of young girls fell ill with convulsions, fever, and spontaneous fits of misbehavior. Unable to determine the cause for these afflictions, a town doctor suggested the girls had been *bewitched*, though they were simply suffering from mild illnesses and in the middle of uncontrolled adolescence. Mass hysteria ensued with hundreds of people jailed under the speculation of them practicing some sort of sorcery. Accusations levied specifically to tarnish good names or contrived as retaliation for opposition to these groundless persecutions continued for a year. Finally, in 1693, the courts ruled against witch hunting and passed a bill to restore the rights and reputations of the affected. However, dreadful deeds had been committed. Sacrificed out of fear and ignorance, human beings had been castigated and condemned.

Today, we want to know. We are laden with a variety of psychic avenues by which we can sneak a magical peek into different areas of our lives. Those who once balked at any mention of spirituality now invite an opportunity to communicate with a deceased loved one. Some inquire about dream jobs and others search for cures for medical maladies. Young women yearn for revelations about Mr. Right and more mature women strive to avoid Mr. Wrong. We have accepted a swarm of television characters, real and fictional, and watch in fascination as they use their clairvoyant skills to conquer crime and life's predicaments. We are astonished as mediums track spiritual nuisances, connecting with those who have made their peaceful transition. Clairvoyants convey messages hidden in our past and intuits soothe our pet's labored soul. In this overwhelming cache of people and information, there is always the possibility of stumbling upon a hoax, scheme, or charlatan. How do we distinguish between who is genuine and who is not, what is real and what isn't?

Astrology

Astrology, numerology, palmistry, and tarot card reading are not psychic aptitudes but sit on the cusp, as tools of the trade. While a psychic can infuse his or her ability into these readings, success lies primarily in being adept in translating the lines on the palm or understanding the significance of numbers or images on the cards. In our modern society, astrology may have paved the way for open dialogue on all things mystic. A popular trend in the 1970s, to some, it made the supernatural seem quite natural. With scientific explanations on how positions of the planets affect the earth and can influence human behavior, astrology became a widely acceptable means of determining human compatibility. *What's your sign* became a usual commencement into any new conversation and everyone from the blue-collar worker, to the Greenwich Villager, to the fabulously wealthy compared sun signs, configuring current and future relationships.

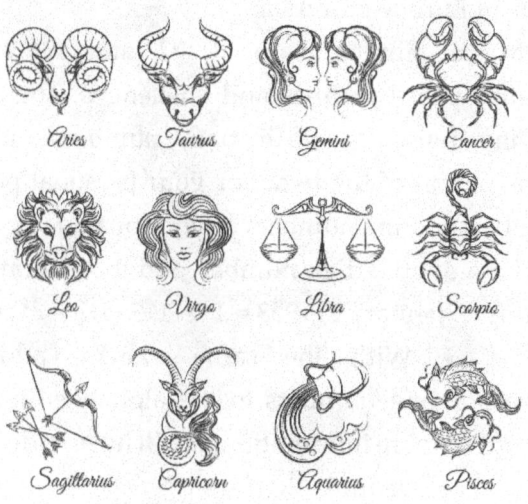

Numerology

An ancient mathematical technique, numerology assigns each alphabet a number and each number, a numeric value. There are power numbers and master numbers, telling of our true potential. Adding the numbers of our birth date or our birth name, we can conclude our natural qualities and traits, leading to our success in life. Some rely on the numbers to dictate when they marry, how many children they will sire, or the profession they will enter, and when. While Pythagoras, Greek philosopher and mathematician, holds credit with devising modern numerology, there is evidence that numerology existed many years prior, in other parts of Europe and Asia.

Master numbers are 11, 22, and 33, which signify special abilities and challenges. There are destiny numbers, birth path numbers, and a combination of the two. For your personal power number, add the numbers of your birth date. If the total is a double-digit number, add those numbers. Example: January 2, 1953 = 1+2+1+9+5+3 = 21, then, 2+1 = 3. With the same system, add all corresponding numbers to the alphabets in your name. For more information, you'll have to do your research. Have fun!

```
1 - A J S    4 - D M V    7 - G P Y
2 - B K T    5 - E N W    8 - H Q Z
3 - C L U    6 - F O X    9 - I R
```

Palmistry

This has been a technique used in Asia and Europe for thousands of years, to determine one's life or prosperity. On our hands, we have smaller lines interacting with the three major lines of the heart, the head, and life. There is the simian crease, a fate line, and bracelets around the wrist. According to those that believe, these lines are self-identifying, revealing the (hi)story of events in our lives. Could they actually be blueprints of our past, present, and future? On two occasions, during psychic readings, my palms were read. Both readers gave information regarding my writing career before I shared with them the fact that I am a writer.

In the 17th century, fingerprints were only part of the human anatomy, not viewed as a means of insight into a person's life. By the 19th century, it was determined that no two people had an exact match of hand or fingerprints. If you look at your own hands, you will see that even those lines differ. You may have similar patterns but all lines, loops, and swirls are uniquely different.

Creating a single identification, this information became useful in legitimizing written contracts. In lieu of a signature, a fingerprint would identify the parties and solidify the agreement. By the latter part of the century, because of this definitive distinction, fingerprints became a prime resource in finding criminal suspects. Today, forensic investigation is an integral part of law enforcement. Any viable print left at any crime scene could lead an investigator to the culprit.

Depending on your source of information, the left hand tells of potential, or the future, and the right, what has already transpired, or, the past.

Some palm readers believe the dominant hand, the one a person writes with, represents the conscious mind and the other, the subconscious mind. Each digit on our hand represent planets or characteristics. Skin texture, shape, and measurements of the hands are also significant, as well as how sinuous they are.

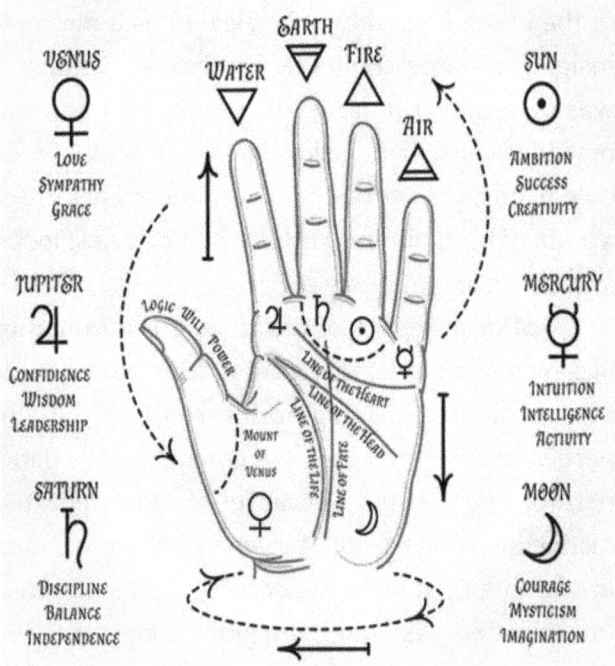

Tarot Cards

Frenchman Etteilla, also known as Jean-Baptiste Attiette (1738-1791), revised the tarot cards and used them in cartomancy, or, divination using a deck of cards. An occultist, he believed that tarot cards derived from the Book of Thoth (the Egyptian god of writing and knowledge) and patterned the themes to mirror ancient Egypt. He used a seventy-eight card deck with two separate parts: the Major Arcana - the greater secrets with twenty-two cards, and the Minor Arcana - the lesser secrets with fifty-six cards. Hand-painted and manufactured sparingly, tarot cards initially provided entertainment only for the upper echelon of European society.

Beginning in the 14th or 15th century as a card game, it has evolved into what it is today, a method for seeing various aspects of one's life, with each card carrying a story, and each story a mirror of the life of the person read. While there is no scientific evidence supporting palmistry or tarot card reading, it is intriguing information.

~ ABILITIES ~

The psychic aptitude perceives all existences. It can review the past, assess the present, and have insight into the future. It is a perspicacity held within one's own personal realm of observation, as one connects with unseen spirits and forces. As we gain awareness of life and self, we develop our capacity at manifesting a more keen perception.

For a psychic, certain information is received, revealed, and processed in particular ways, specific to one's ability to recognize the data. In my discovery of the spirit world, I have found that psychic ability comes in a variety of appearances and that not all psychics are equal. That is, we are not all versed in the same areas of spiritual guidance and not all to the same extent. Here are several areas of psychic ability. Do you see yourself?

- Clairsentience: the ability to feel another's emotions.
- Clairaudience: the ability to hear beyond your immediate realm.
- Clairescence: a keen sense of smell, without the scent being in the air.
- Claircognizance: intrinsic knowing.

- Clairgustance: a keen sense of taste, without having the particular substance in your mouth.
- Clairvoyance: the ability to see what is not apparent, through the mind's eye.

~ AUTHENTICITY ~

Questionable, of course, are those who capitalize on natural curiosity and human insecurities by charging exorbitant sitting fees to share their *gift* of perception. I understand the need to make a living and can appreciate the desire to accomplish this by doing what one is skilled to do. However, an honest heart must be the impetus or it can defeat the purpose (of helping others). My own contact with those with extraordinary insight has been largely positive though I have come across more than one person who was either not as efficient in psychic ability or not psychic at all.

Summer, 1976

I am always on the prowl for proof of the things I don't understand or don't believe, to help me decide what may, or may not, be true. In 1976, at nineteen years old, spending a leisurely summer's day in New York City, I met a psychic. I had never encountered one before, at least, not that I was aware. The woman claimed to be a fortuneteller. It wasn't a numinous meeting. She was lurking the streets for clients, and most likely saw *easy mark* written all over my naïve face.

Probably younger than her fiftyish appearance, she dressed the part of the axiomatic Gypsy woman. She wrapped her hair with a large scarf and wore a long ruffled skirt, with a long-sleeved white blouse and black vest over that. It was all indicative of the aura of her being knowledgeable in spirits and life. In particular, *my* life. To confirm her position, the woman pointed to a neon sign attached to a second floor window. It flashed and beckoned potential customers to have their palms read for just a few dollars. I was not as interested in knowing my future as I was in finding out if this palm reading/fortunetelling business was valid. Ever the pessimist seeking to be an optimist, I had to try.

Ushered upstairs, a crystal ball sat in the middle of a table. I had only seen one on TV and was always skeptical of its proclaimed power. How could a glass ball have information about people? I wanted to see this. I had to see it, if I was going to believe it. I waited for misty images to emanate inside of it but it didn't. I never saw a thing. The woman, however, was getting all kinds of vibes and phantasmagorias. She was saying this and insisting on that about my life but none of it was germane to me. At least, I didn't see it. And, by now, I realized I had allowed myself to be in the secluded company of a stranger, in an unfamiliar place. It was time to leave.

As I stood to make my exit, the woman instructed me to return the following day, to get more information on my future. I was to bring more money (ha!) and an egg. *An egg?* First, how was that going to happen on a bus from Jersey to New York City? Figuring the least resistance would allow me the most uneventful exit, I agreed. *Yeah. Sure.* Hurrying past a man I had not noticed until just then, I rushed down the stairs, onto the sweet pavement of Manhattan. I never returned.

Mulling over this experience to include in this book, I researched the significance of the egg as it may have related to my experience. I found that it is part of a confidence scheme. The client/victim's perfectly fine egg, switched at some point during the reading with a rotten one, becomes the disclosure of ill will. Cracked open, its decayed matter pours out, producing a warning from the teller: the client/victim has been afflicted with a curse by who-knows-who, from who-knows-where, about who-knows-what. Though there are no specifics, there is, for a nominal fee, a cure. As the teller gains the confidence of the client/victim, the money cycle repeats for as long as the client/victim allows.

January 2014

On a quest to learn more about the world of psychic abilities and my place within it, I signed up for an Intensive Psychic Development seminar. The advertisement of a full and interesting itinerary had caught my attention. For three days, and for several hundred dollars, this symposium was to include impromptu psychic readings and an exercise on tarot card reading. By virtue of the title of the course, I had high expectations. I anticipated being in the presence of other psychics, with various levels of ability, sharing knowledge and information. While the class certainly had its pleasant moments, it did not live up to its promotion.

Most partakers in this course had no background in psychic ability, so there was little exchange of information. Spontaneous readings were suddenly no longer part of the agenda, however, for a nominal fee, participants could sign up for private sessions afterwards. The tarot card lesson was nothing more than entertainment.

Participants selected one card after another, until a more congenial, more agreeable, one appeared. With chief aspects of this program changed, the ads seemed only a lure. When asked about the changes in the advertised schedule, the resident psychic shared that her spirit guides were steering her in other directions. Hmmm... I was, indeed, dubious. It smelled of deception. To be fair, others enjoyed the course and their time spent. I still say, be wary.

With many frauds to filter through, know that a (true) psychic has no need for gimmicks or props. Their eyes will not roll back into their heads, well, not usually, and lights will not necessarily flicker. Most likely, you will not hear conversations in unfamiliar languages or see anyone levitating. Regarding insights to your future, whatever revelations you receive, understand that you remain in control of your life/destiny, over how true those disclosures become. Any prediction does not supersede the action/inaction one takes after the reading. If the cause (the action) changes, so changes the effect (the result).

Not everyone will leave a psychic reading prepared to make dramatic, life-altering changes. You may not instantly recognize, or be able to relate to, some information given. It may take time for some of what you hear to come to completion and then, only with sufficient causes will certain effects manifest. I have had readings proven true as much as two years afterwards. If you are considering a psychic reading, choose your reader wisely. If you have a wide circle of friends and associates, you may (surprisingly) find a good psychic recommendation amongst them.

~ IS THE WHOLE WORLD PSYCHIC? ~

Are we all born with psychic attributes? How does this work? Are there really *chosen ones*? Is it in our DNA?

How many times have you felt a presence you could not see or had the experience of knowing what was going to happen prior to it occurring? What of that urgent feeling telling you that *something* is not right? Your mind is on fire, though you cannot tell exactly what this something is. You follow your intuition (or not), and *BAM!* That something happens. Perhaps, engaged in daily living, you suddenly begin to feel that what is happening with you at that precise moment has happened before. However, you know that you have never been to *this* specific location, with *that* particular person, partaking in these *exact* series of motions. Yet, simultaneous to it happening, you remember every movement. It seems like a dream within reality or reality within a dream. Either way, you exclaim, *I knew it! I knew it!* Well, how did you know?

> *Déjà vu: An awareness of a moment that, as far as your conscious mind is concerned, has never occurred.*

I recently went on a family excursion to a children's museum. We walked around, looking at the exhibits and participating in fun activities. Entering the IMAX theatre, a feeling of knowing crept into my senses. Though it was my first visit, I knew this theatre. But, when? I sat quietly, so that I could embrace this moment of familiarity. I wanted to become in-tune with all movement. I didn't know the other family who had wandered in but I knew they would place their baby's stroller where they had just placed it. I knew they would sit where they were now sitting. How did I know?

Savannah, the oldest city in the state of Georgia, has a rich history of antebellum structures, plantations, and of ghostly hauntings. Ebony and Erica are two young ladies who recently visited. While out on a casual walking tour, they passed an auditorium, whose open doors invited in any passersby. Erica peeked in, saw an average auditorium, and kept walking. Ebony, however, passed by and waved, speaking to someone inside in a *Hey Girl!* kind of way. Curious, Erica stopped and looked back at Ebony and asked who she was speaking to. Ebony said that she was responding to a woman who had waved to her from the stage area. Since this was a tour, they thought the woman might be preparing for a play. They went inside to find her, to get more information, but the place was empty.

Ebony described the woman as being dressed in a white with blue trim, dated dress, similar to what slaves wore during that period. She was dark skinned, with her brown hair braided and tucked up. They searched for this woman, for anyone who could confirm her existence. There was no one around. Was this a lingering spirit, still attached to a time and place long gone?

Extra Sensory Perception: Perceptions that involve awareness of information of people and events external to oneself; second sight.

Most people travel in the outer layer of psychic ability. This is where we cultivate our skills to recognize and assess basic human qualities and frailties, as well as various conditions and circumstances in our environment. With repetitive interaction, we acquaint ourselves with human tendencies. Our instincts become sharper and recurring encounters become indelibly logged in our minds. We create automatic mental conclusions of these consistent behaviors. That is, we come to know the outcome of situations based upon prior engagement. These are what I consider external assessments. A wisdom developed from life experience.

Internal assessments are spiritual insights that discern specific inner life conditions. Human or not, every existence has energy and each of these energies has a history that goes beyond what can be ordinarily perceived. With the ability to see further than our basic, preliminary observations, a psychic can see all that has been, all that is, or all that will be.

So, are we all psychic? Do we all carry this potential? I believe we all possess some level of intuition, with the possibility of excelling beyond our perceived limitations. However, I'm not certain that we all have the capacity to manifest the qualities of a psychic. It would be similar to saying that we could all become master musicians. We may all love music but some will have careers as artists producing superlative compositions while others will have to be content with only listening.

It becomes a matter of one's mission and being able to create and develop one's circumstances.

For various reasons, we are not all going to execute and accomplish the same objectives, attain them with the same methods, or to the same degree. And that's okay. While we have many similarities as human beings, our differences is what gives rise to who we are as individuals. It directs us towards our unique purpose. Therefore, I believe we are all masterful at *some*thing. Just not the *same* thing.

4 FAMILY AFFAIRS

Most of my immediate family is a cross between believers and sort-of believers. We survive the *real* world by being sensible but won't hesitate to sit, in wide-eyed wonder, and listen to any ghost story. We have all had our experiences, individually and collectively. Looking back, strange, questionable things had always occurred around us.

In the very early 1980s, when I lived in New Jersey, objects placed in one space and found in another occurred frequently enough that I began thinking someone was gaining access to my apartment. Nothing stolen. Items only moved. I thought about it from a physical aspect, not a spiritual one, and ignored these episodes. I didn't want to think about seeing silhouettes sitting at the edge of my bed, waking me with its presence. One would think that having psychic abilities would make me composed with the supernatural, but it doesn't. I still cover my eyes during a thriller movie and quiver when imagining myself driving down a dark, vacant country road.

Several years after our move southward, my sons and my niece, Tai, saw the shadow of a man in a top hat walking across the carport, passing by the kitchen door. We have all heard the noises. It took some years in my new home before I considered the possibility of it being anything other than the house settling. At one point, I would hear bumps underneath my home so much that I thought someone had taken up residence there. Asleep, I have opened my eyes to telephone cords swinging, knocking against my nightstand, just inches from my head. There was no one around. I have watched my bedroom door slowly close, with nothing around to cause the movement. At least, nothing I could see. Yes, at times, it got spooky.

Occasionally, as I walked around my home, I would get the strongest sensation someone was behind me. It would make my neck and back prickle. One night, I saw the silhouette of someone I thought was my youngest son, standing in the upstairs hall. He (it) vanished just as my son walked from another room on the first floor. Not smitten with just blood relations, spirits have revealed themselves to our visitors. On separate visits, two of my son's friends reported seeing the apparition of a little boy dressed in clothing from the 17th century, standing in his bedroom closet. Both were unnerved. One did not return for many years. We could never pinpoint any particular reason the spirits would appear. They just did.

~ THE MIST ~

In 1993, I was still in stages of denial. I had developed a comfort in being spiritually ignorant. However, out of my peripheral vision, I started seeing what I can only describe as an opaque mist. It glided a few inches or so from the floor in my bedroom and the moment I turned to look, it would disappear around a corner or simply melt into the air. I decided this was a result of my poor vision but, at the back of my mind, I was not so confident. I didn't want to acknowledge it but couldn't completely fool myself into believing it was an optical illusion.

Over the course of the next several months, the mist appeared frequently enough that I started making mental notes to determine the precise moment it would appear and what could be causing it. Until I had an answer, until I understood what I was seeing, I couldn't mention it to anyone. Never drawing any conclusions, this year rolled into the next.

Summer 1994

While my family vacationed in Europe for several weeks, I stayed home alone. Working in law enforcement had made me security conscious and every night I performed a ritual of double-checking every window and door, then activating the alarm. At the end of the first week, with my security check complete, I settled down for the evening. I am not certain how much time had lapsed before I was startled awake, unable to breathe. I also could not move. Everything looked dull and misty, in black and white, similar to a film noir. I could see the dim night light in the hall and two panels of my lace window curtains billowing towards me, as though a night's breeze was pushing them inward. It seemed as though my conscious mind and my subconscious mind were active and interacting. I was awake, but not awake. Aware, but did not know what was happening.

Lying in bed, I could feel something pressing against my face. Though I could not see it, it was the reason I could not breathe. There was an intense presence with me and I had to figure out how to overcome it. My only thought was prayer. I was certain it could cut through whatever was trying to shut down my respiratory system. And it did. The darkness lifted.

My heart raced as my eyes scanned the room for some sign of what had happened. There was nothing. Everything was intact and still. The curtains hung motionless, just as they should have. I realized later that with the windows closed they could not have moved the way I had seen them moving. Easing out of my stupor, I quickly gathered my thoughts. Was there someone in my home? It was the only way I could explain any of it. If there was anyone here, he was not getting away. Reaching for my weapon, I got up and cautiously searched one room at a time. Top to bottom, and up again.

There was nothing. There was no one. Every door and window, locked. In subsequent days, I busied myself so I would not think about this experience. I slept with the lights on, hoping it could ward off all supernatural phenomena (a childhood myth). I couldn't tell anyone. With no physical evidence, no proof, I wasn't comfortable sharing this. I could not put my credibility on the line for something I could not explain.

It was several weeks after my family returned from their overseas trip that I confided in my mother. Her response was a surprise. This woman, whom I had known all my life, was now telling me that she had been having experiences with spirits in our home for quite some time. Her resolution had always been to invite them to sit and pray with her. I was speechless. Why had she never told me? It was simple. She didn't want to cause me any panic. Well, she missed the mark on that one.

One evening, many years later, I mustered enough courage to execute my own experiment. I had been reading a book that had instructions on how to manifest spirits. It didn't seem difficult and there was nothing about conjuring evil spirits. I would have never done that. Everything about this was about goodness... the color of the candle, my thoughts, and the energy. And I had everything I needed. The white candle and a mirror. No one was home, it was quiet. I decided to try.

I lit a white candle and placed it in front of a large mirror. I turned off the lights and sat in front, slowing my breath, becoming peaceful. I didn't close my eyes because I wanted to see what, if anything, would happen. Looking at the candle reflecting in the mirror, I began asking if there were any spirits around me. If there were, show yourselves. It didn't take long at all. A midst began forming around the candle. I could clearly see it in the mirror. That was as far as my mettle would take me. I turned on the light, snuffed out the candle, and put everything away. I got what I needed: proof.

~ PET SPIRITS ~

Animals are instinctual creatures and our beloved dogs occasionally tuned in to the energies floating around our home. They would sit in a room and look towards the ceiling, moving their heads from one side to the other, following some unseen object. They have rushed up the stairs to a bedroom, as though responding to someone calling their name. Sometimes they would sit obediently, as if obeying an order. Had I not witnessed these moments, I may not have thought much about their spirituality or mortality.

When my sons were too young to stay home by themselves, we ran every household errand together. One day, rather than endure another trip to the grocery store, my oldest son asked to stay home. At ten years old, he was mature and responsible enough to be alone for a minimal amount of time. After reviewing our safety checklist and asking a neighbor to keep watch, the rest of the family drove the few minutes to the store. Purchasing just a few items, we promptly returned home, just in time to see my son bounding out of the house, baseball bat slung over his shoulder. He was startled. Was there an intruder?

The story goes that while in his room reading, my son had heard the footsteps of a dog running up the stairs. There were plastic runners on the carpet then, making any contact more audible. Peeking out into the hall, my son saw nothing. Not only was no one else supposed to be in our home, it had been many months since we had had a dog. Grabbing his bat, he ran outside for safety. Not one for delusional thoughts or hysterical outbursts, I knew something had happened. While everyone waited outside, I searched our home. There was no one inside and no signs that anyone had been there.

Some months prior, our terrier had disappeared from the backyard. When he didn't return, we assumed he had met with his demise. Now, we thought, he may have come back to visit. In spirit form.

Our Labrador retriever was rambunctious and fiercely protective. No one could walk by our home without her barking ferociously, warning everyone away. Dashing from the backyard into the three-foot high crawlspace underneath the house, she would race to the front. Her bark would blast through the wire-covered vent, out into the street, reverberating through the neighborhood. After six years, she had become overly aggressive and unpredictable. After an attack on my youngest son, I made the emotional decision to euthanize her. In a room at the veterinarian's office, I held her in my arms well past the moment she transitioned. Afterwards, on occasion, I would hear her bark echoing through the house, from the crawlspace underneath.

~ GHOST BUSTING ~

When my youngest son was 18 years old, he told me that he had been sharing space with spirits from the time he was a child. *Figures* was what he called them and many of his encounters were with negative energies. Not knowing this, I had always taken a stern approach to his difficult behavior, banishing him to his room. I now found that this was the very space the spirits would gather to taunt him.

I remembered the times he explained away his constant violations of house rules as the devil (yes, that again) prompting him to do wrong. I recalled finding the word *help* carved on the window ledge and scribbled in his workbook. He had no answers for me then but now my son said there had been an unseen force compelling him to write the word. I had no idea there were spirits causing this kind of mayhem. I was not in belief mode then, when it came to paranormal activity, and neglected to see his distress. Now, I did not dispute his claims. And I wished I had been more embracing of him and the spirit world. But it was a new day. Now, we had a common ground on which we could establish some sort of camaraderie.

As we explored spiritual phenomenon, to maintain a high level of integrity, I made a conscious effort to keep our encounters with the spirits honest. If we shared a ghostly experience, so that my assertions would not be an influence on him, I would ask my son a vague question and have him elaborate. This worked well and we constantly validated our abilities and confirmed the many spirits roaming our home. One evening, as we watched TV in the living room, I saw the imprint of a face protruding from my older son's bedroom door. I was astounded. It was similar to pin art and I had never seen anything like it. The deep, dark brown color of the door gave it a foreboding quality. I couldn't imagine anything that could be causing this and thought it was an illusion. I calmly asked my younger son to look at the door and tell me what he saw. I gave no indication of what I was looking at and I hoped he would say it was just an ordinary door. Immediately, he said he could see a face coming out of it.

We had seen the very same thing so there was no way it didn't happen. An energy was manipulating an inanimate object to manifest itself. It was chilling. My nerves did not allow me to investigate. I turned off the television and my son and I left the room. I could not pretend any kind of bravado to see what was on the other side of that door. Of course, when my older son returned home we told him of our latest spiritual encounter. I even offered him a move back upstairs, to his old room, but he declined. Unconcerned, he went on with his life as usual, sleeping in the dark, with the door closed. It was unbelievable to me that he could be so calm. Cool as a cucumber. Until…

Early one morning, my unflappable offspring ran upstairs to my room, his blanket bundled around him. He wasn't a kid anymore. He was a strong, confident young man who was now shivering with concern. He had woken to a face staring at him from the foot of his bed. Describing it as the face of death, it was there specifically for him. And he was not ready to go. Was it the same spirit in the door? I don't know. And I had no desire to find out.

Surprisingly, even this experience did not alter my son's perspective. He was not afraid of the spiritual realm and would not allow those supernatural energies to dictate how he lived his life. He resumed sleeping in the dark, with the door closed, unperturbed at our spiritual shenanigans.

~ SPIRIT CLEANSING ~

Some of our spirits came with scents attached or would appear only during certain times. There was a spirit we called Lamont, who was a kind and unruffled character. He appeared only when my youngest son composed new age or jazz music, melodies that, obviously, soothed all spirits. When

Lamont was present, we would get whiffs of burning tobacco throughout the house. He never ventured outside of my son's room and stayed for only a short while, leaving as quietly as he appeared.

In the late evening, many times after I had gone to bed, energies would arrive to pester my youngest son. On a few occasions, a spirit would be such a strong presence that he would wake me and, for lack of any better term, we would have to exorcise it. Not that we were experts at it. We were not. We knew nothing about purging spirits. We did know, however, that we had to get them out of the house and were confident that prayer was the answer.

Friday, January 25, 2002 12 am

Having to report for work at 8:30 am and sometimes being on-call overnight, midnight ghost busting had become disruptive. However, one spirit was so commanding that it caused my body to tingle. It had to go.

It was a Caucasian male, with a broad chest and shoulders, wearing a Confederate soldier's uniform. With his hat on, he stood straight and tall. He was a powerful spirit. With a blanket wrapped loosely around my shoulders, I could feel its chill. In my right ear, I heard praying, a millisecond out of rhythm with me. I had a sensation that the spirit was inside of my blanket, trying to get inside of my physical self. It was an unusual feeling and something I would not allow.

Up until this moment, I did not believe in spirit possession. I rejected any thought of it. Not because of any scientific reason. Or any religious one. I was afraid. I had seen The Exorcist and that infamous, gut-spitting, head-turning, horrendous scene. I was not interested in knowing anything about that. It was too eerie to think about, let alone seriously research. I wanted no part of it. I fanned out the blanket, dispersing the energy with prayer. *Not here!* The fight did not last long. Within seconds, the entity melded into the air.

Tuesday, February 26, 2002 9:20 pm

There was another energy in the house. With great focus, I sent my prayers and my determination into each room of the house, to rid us of this spirit. It had gone into the den and up to the loft. Sitting there on boxes, it was hiding in fear. I had never encountered timidity in a spirit and felt a bit of empathy for it. But not enough to allow it to stay. It had to leave. It floated out of our house and melted into the wall of a neighbor's home.

My son and I debriefed. He was first to report, describing the exact path I had taken to expel the spirit. Looking towards the window, he could also see, with his mind's eye, that the energy was on the move again. Walking in and out of other homes, it walked towards the top of the street. I tuned in and we both saw a male spirit going into Dustin's home. The next day, not wanting to rattle the neighborhood, my son and I said nothing. However, confirmation came. In a conversation about the paranormal, Dustin shared that he had seen a male ghost in his home the night before.

We had an incident where my (then) four-year-old nephew Kaleb's visit ended with a missing toy. Content with entertaining himself with cartoons on TV, he had his Ninja Turtle action figure by his side. I saw it. When it was time for him to leave, it was nowhere around. He was too young to play paranormal mind games with me and the only option was that something had moved it. There had been an extensive search. Each room simultaneously combed through by three adults. Nothing. As Kaleb and his mother walked to the front door, I glanced into the living room. *Poof!* There it was. In a space that had been searched and walked through by several people.

Was this our psyche (the unconscious and conscious mind), playing mind games with itself? Was it scotoma, a mental block, causing us to overlook it because we had convinced ourselves it was lost? I don't know. It could have been either of those things, or neither of them. What I do know is that we searched for the toy and couldn't find it. Then, in plain sight, it was there.

~ THE SHADOW ~

On Saturday, October 29, 2005, I purchased a new camcorder with infrared capabilities. My son had been feeling a presence in his room and we were curious to know if we could record it. Hoping we could seize this energy on film, we set up the new ghost hunting equipment in my bedroom. This provided the best view of the upstairs hall. We could catch anything entering or leaving any of the rooms. Having resumed our normal activity, in less than thirty minutes my son walked out of his room, breathless. It was there. It had left and returned. He didn't see it but he could feel it.

We immediately stopped recording and watched. In the shape of a boomerang, it was quick, but it was there. To preserve the experience, I copied the video to a disc and made still photos. Unfortunately, the photographs lose clarity in print but I've included them anyway, to give you an idea of this phenomenal moment captured.

In description, it was a dark kind of mist but the bottom corner of a picture frame on the wall was visible through it. The energy initially emerged as a small blur and as it came further out of the room, took on the shape of a boomerang or something spreading its wings. It made a quick dip downward and, in a sweeping motion, went back in the direction it came. It happened in an instant. And then, it was gone.

Confirming this spirit in my home was remarkable. It was also a bit disconcerting. On the one hand, we obtained incredible footage and proof. On the other, this energy was in my personal space and I wasn't so delighted about that.

I realize that you have only my word on this. I can only tell you that I was there, throughout the entire process. I made the purchase of the camcorder and tape cassette. I assisted in setting up and documenting this occurrence. I was the only human being near the equipment during the time the entity appeared and was recorded. Viewed immediately afterwards, there was no time for manipulation.

I also visually dissected this particular area of my home, attempting to find the flaw, the illusion. I checked for refractions or any possible way light could have passed through closed window blinds and curtains, reflecting on the wall. I performed a variety of motions, trying to recreate this movement, to find an alternative. I could not do it. This was, in my estimation, proof of unseen energy navigating through my home. It was of a supernatural, paranormal, kind.

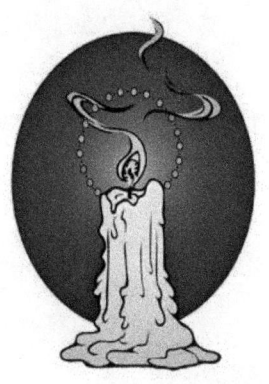

5 SPIRITS IN MY MIDST

Who can unequivocally say that there is no such thing as this or that, sending supernatural incidences into an abyss of refutation? There is not one person who could know everything. I have learned that denial does not modify what is, and our motions to suppress truth will only prolong the learning process. And while I can always question someone else's experience and declaration, it is difficult to deny my own.

*Supernatural: an order of existence
beyond what is ordinarily visible.*

Who, or what, is *Spirit*? I have heard others speak of it as the source of great wisdom and light, providing certain information at a specific time, about precise things. They say, *Spirit said* this or *Spirit said* that, guiding them here or there. Usually it is referencing an invisible entity, outside of oneself. Perhaps we attribute the qualities of Spirit to something other than ourselves because we do not always recognize that we are the embodiment of this higher state of consciousness. And if Spirit resides within each of us, is the knowledge we receive a manifestation of our own enlightened nature that already knows and understands?

I aspire to be a spiritual being, one that utilizes the theory and understanding of life, in its entire splendor, on its deepest level. I'd like to believe in all energies in the universe, with every piece connecting to all pieces. I'd like to live unafraid, unhindered by my knowledge. But I often have no immediate answers and may be, for the moment, more bewildered than at ease.

~ PRAYER ~

I have found that while in prayer, I am more open to energies of the deceased traversing the universe. Not that I ever wanted to be. I didn't. I have had no desire to see death or the spirit state of anyone deceased. But I have also had little choice.

Ben

In the very late 1990s, my sons and I made a trip to New Jersey during their summer vacation. I was going to use it as a parenting moment, an opportunity to show my offspring where I grew up, maybe have them realize how fortunate they were, blah, blah, blah. That didn't happen, but it was a revealing time for my abilities.

A longtime family friend, Ben, had been hospitalized, ill with cancer. It had been more than fifteen years since I had seen him and now, he was gravely ill.

On a Wednesday evening, I accompanied his wife to the hospital. Once robust, Ben had lost much of his weight. His head of dark hair was now grey, but his smile was still broad. The chemotherapy made it difficult to keep his skin moisturized and he thanked me for the virgin olive oil I had brought for him. There was another visitor there and a makeshift Buddhist altar stood against the wall, facing the bed. Together, we offered prayers for Ben's good health and happiness. It wasn't long before unsolicited visions, in my mind's eye, began.

Ben was dressed in a black hooded cloak and bent over. I could not see his face, but there was a deep sense of knowing, from the center of my own being, regarding this scene that was transpiring. There was no doubt I was seeing Ben. Two spirits of higher consciousness, also dressed in black cloaks, held him under either of his arms. They walked him towards the altar, *into the light* were the words offered to me. There was a feeling of an embrace and I received the knowledge: *his body is weak but his spirit is strong.* Keeping my head still, with only my eyes, I glanced at the others in the room. No one was having any reaction to indicate hearing or seeing what I was hearing and seeing. The experience was only for me.

I didn't know where this information was coming from but it was clear. I had seen Ben's death. Though he wanted to live, physically, his body would not last. He would not be with us much longer. I was stunned at this revelation. This wasn't something I wanted to know, certainly nothing I felt compelled to share. However, in the air, there was an energy revealing a sadness that needed tending. After our prayers, wanting to be truthful, but not the bearer of devastating news, I chose my words carefully. It would be the last time I would see Ben, so I had to share what I had received. I had not communicated with him in more than a decade and did not know how this information pertained to his circumstance. I didn't know anything about his connections with other people or if he would understand what I had to say. I only knew that I had to speak these words to him.

Just as I had heard it, I gently told Ben that I knew of his strong will to survive, to defeat his illness. Instantly, he wept. He thanked me, saying that some of the people around him had questioned his determination to live. They judged his hospitalization as a defeat of his spirit rather than a deterioration of his body. Through his tears, Ben said that no one knew of his struggle, of his deep physical pain. They didn't know of the courage he had to develop to face his life, even if it meant in death. It stung his heart to know that anyone would think he had lost his resolve to live. He thanked me profusely for understanding this about him.

I left the hospital with mixed emotions. I knew I would never see Ben again but there was comfort in knowing I had offered him a level of peace, that he knew that someone understood his heart. When I returned home, I documented this incident in my journal and called Angel, another longtime friend who also knew Ben. I told her of my revelation, of seeing Ben's death. I shared with her my uneasiness with it. To keep us both in a positive position Angel said she believed he would live. That was my hope too.

A couple of weeks later Angel called. Ben had passed. I was glad to have had that time with him. And my question remains: how could I have visualized his death?

Mrs. D

One evening, I inadvertently found myself attending a memorial service at a local community center. I did not know Mrs. D but I did know her son, and stayed to offer prayers for her eternal happiness.

There was a table, with a photo of a refined woman dressed in black. As prayers began, to my left appeared the image of a woman dressed in a long, simply cut, grey flowing dress with a splash of a light red material gracefully floating about her head and shoulders. She was gloriously happy, smiling and dancing. Addressing her family, sitting at the front of the gathering, she was overjoyed to see them together and wished them happiness in many lifetimes to come. She listened to the praying and smiled, *I have to do that next time*. Though she was not Buddhist, she wished that they would all, at some point, take on the Buddhist faith. She danced from one side of the platform to the other and quieted down. She laid down in mid-air, closed her eyes, tucked her chin to her chest, and laid herself to rest. She was gone.

No one around me seemed to be sharing these moments. When it was time for the eulogy, the family stood, one by one, to express their love, respect, and appreciation for their matriarch. They described her as a happy, fun-loving woman, who loved life and enjoyed dancing. They described very same woman I had seen.

Tuesday, September 11, 2001

It was 8:30 am. A police detective, I reported to the Criminal Investigations Division, Tucker Precinct. It started as a typical multitasking morning. I talked with the secretary, helped answer phone calls, responded to my own messages, and shuffled paperwork. It was customary to have the television on, programmed to CNN or any news station. This particular morning was no different. It was an ordinary day, listening to commentaries and a weather broadcast from New York. I periodically looked at the TV screen. At one glance, there was a live aerial view of Manhattan's tall buildings. Then, an airplane glided into one of the World Trade Center towers, causing an explosion.

My mind did not register what my eyes had just seen. I wondered if someone had switched channels and we were now watching a movie. But it didn't look like a film. It looked like live footage. I couldn't make any sense of it. The secretary broke my daze with her shouts of, *"That was real! That was real!"* It was unbelievable and one of the most horrific acts and attacks against humanity. We listened throughout the day, as reports came in, piecing together these tragic moments of terrorism.

David and Mrs. Ellis

David had perished in the first plane to hit the Twin Towers in New York. He was also a Nichiren Buddhist. To honor his life, there was to be simultaneous memorial services for him at various Buddhist community centers across the country. The entire membership felt the emotional reverberation of such an atrocity. Though I did not know David, I attended his service on Saturday, September 15, 2001. At 5 pm, I offered my sincerest respect and prayers for his eternal happiness.

When I arrived at the Atlanta center, Mrs. Ellis was sitting close to the front of this assembly. I sat further back with her daughter Pearl, who was sitting with her father. Mrs. Ellis had known David for many years and Pearl was concerned about the emotional effect the service may have on her. While she stayed with her father, she asked that I sit with her mother. She must have thought it strange that I declined.

Pearl didn't know that memorial services had become prime time for paranormal activity for me. Still in the throes of trying to understand this spirit/psychic world, I wasn't so excited about seeing dead people. This new avenue of perception opened unexpectedly and I thought that if I could be spiritually unapproachable, the spirits would pass me by. I didn't know what the criteria was for these kinds of situations but I had to find a way to be spiritually incognito, if there was such a thing. But Pearl, not wanting her mother to sit alone during this sensitive tribute, made a second appeal. I could not continue to refuse. How prophetic it was that there was only one seat available. Beside Mrs. Ellis.

Death is a natural part of the cycle of birth, aging, and demise. One can live a long life or a short one, and time is relative to karma. We may think a loved one has *gone too soon* but, in reality, they passed when it was their time to pass, when the conditions in their life created that moment. I understood and believed in this perspective but I had questions concerning the circumstance in which David had lost his life. I wondered why he had died in such a tragic manner, given his life of serving others. I searched for my answers in prayer and the visions came quickly.

Going back in time, I became part of this fiery event. The plane approached the blaze from my left side. With a clear view, I watched as David sat in an aisle seat, bracing himself for impact. With people seated behind him and to the right of him, I could feel his strong life force. It said that he understood his life, that he understood his death, and that he had accomplished his mission. There was no fear.

The plane began its descent into perpetuity. Anticipating the full arrival of the aircraft and its passengers, the flames burned fiercely. I was beginning to feel the heat. My body temperature had risen and I felt faint. My face felt flushed with the warmth of the event I was seeing. As the plane moved closer to the fire, I became anxious and more heated. I felt a need to brace myself. I was going into the fire. I was going to burn.

I wanted to reach out for help. I wanted to get up and run away from the calamity. It seemed that I was in a time warp, experiencing two dimensions, conscious of both. In the *real* world, I was alert, aware of my surroundings, and I was safe. There was no fire. My spirit, however, was involved in this incident. It was transferring to my physical being and the high temperature from that was becoming unbearable. Mindful of being in front of other people, I had to control myself. If I followed my impulse to jump up and run from a fire no one else could see, I would seem a crazed woman. And I did not want to be that.

I had to extricate myself from the event. I had to stop this vision. But how? I had never done this. Following my instincts, I willfully shut down my mind's eye. I shut out the blaze. Disconnected from the revelation. I returned to reality, as I knew it. After the service, before we could go our separate ways, I spoke with Mrs. Ellis. I felt that I could trust her and shared my experience. Her response was unexpected. She said it was an unusual experience for her too. In the midst of offering prayers, for no reason she could think of, she had felt intense heat on her left ear, as though it was burning. The plane, in this spiritual setting, traveled from her left. She had felt what I had seen.

Mrs. Harris

In her 70s when she passed, Mrs. Harris, in my opinion, was a quiet and refined woman. Paying my respects, I attended her memorial service. She appeared in my mind's eye relaxed, enjoying jazz music, saying, *I'm cool*. It was a humorous image because she didn't seem a *cool* kind of person. However, I spoke with her daughter after the service and found that Mrs. Harris was, actually, a jazz lover, someone with a zest for life. It wasn't unusual to see her snapping her fingers in time, savoring the music. She was, actually, cool.

Griffin

A young man in his 30s, I did not know Griffin or anything about how he had lived. I only knew that his physical life had ended. On Tuesday, January 22, 2002, I attended his memorial service in support of his mother. Watching Mrs. G grieve over the loss of her only child, I prayed to guide his energy to her, so that he could console her. Griffin refused. There was no desire to appear, to wrap his spirit around his mother. He was severely, emotionally, distant from her.

In prayer, I could see Griffin as a boy, wearing a long sleeved white shirt, carrying a briefcase. He was wandering around in circles, not very happy. The word I received was *lost*. Particularly because I had never met Griffin, I did not know how to interpret my vision. However, his mother's eulogy of him confirmed his life.

A child prodigy, Griffin had left home at the age of fourteen years old to live in the dormitory of a local university. Making a life for himself, he never returned home to live. Mrs. G described her son as a boy, walking around under the hot summer sun, wearing long sleeved shirts, buttoned to the top, carrying his briefcase. Just as I had seen.

Suffering with depression, over the past several years Griffin had been deeply troubled. Nevertheless, his mother believed that just prior to his death, his spirit had lifted. She believed he had found happiness. Understanding that she wanted to remember her son in this bright light, I kept my visions to myself. It was the proper thing to do.

~ A SÉANCE ~

Despite my personal experiences with the spirit world, I continued to believe in a limited sort of way. I still questioned much of it. Maybe it was my way of staying balanced and feeling sane. When it came to séances, I had always been a non-believer.

It was an interesting thought, communicating with someone who has passed along into the universe, but I wasn't sure it was real. I had seen the hijinks on television, of pictures shaking off the walls and milky mists squirming around. It was all surely created by camera techniques. There was always a psychic talking with a spirit, linking it to a participant in the room. It all seemed contrived but with minimal experience, I couldn't absolutely say it wasn't true.

While trying to maintain an open mind, I had one stipulation regarding séances, past life regression, or anything that involved possible transference of spirit: I would not participate with strangers. I had to feel safe. I had to trust that no one would open spiritual doors I could not close. When the opportunity arose to partake in a séance with someone I was familiar with, I did.

I had known Lynn for several years. Outspoken on life and all of its prospects, I didn't always agree with her perspectives but was always intrigued enough to listen. As my personal spiritual progress would have it, her sister was a master psychic.

I met Marlo at Lynn's house one evening and our conversation took a natural turn towards mysticism. I listened intently as she talked about the many aspects of her psychic gift. In turn, she graciously listened to the few experiences I had had. During our talk, my third eye opened. I was seeing Marlo lying on a hospital bed, ill. And there was a strong connection with African culture. I felt encouraged to share this information with her.

Marlo confirmed a hospital stay. Released earlier in the day, she was staying with Lynn while she recuperated. She also shared her predilection for African art. We talked for a long while and when the evening was done, we promised to stay in touch. Marlo had conducted séances in the past and we planned to get together for that purpose. I was excited, sure, but I had a few legitimate concerns before possibly opening my home to any adverse energies:

Question #1: What is a séance?
Answer: An avenue to communicate with the dead.
Question #2: What do I do during a séance?
Answer: Be willing to be a conduit.
Question #3: What if a malevolent entity attempts to stay in my home.
Answer: Our own spirits would be strong enough to banish any evil.
Question #3: Would I be in a trance?
Answer: Probably not.
Question #4: Would I be possessed?
Answer: I certainly hope not.

Sunday, November 23, 2003

Though there were no guarantees, this was too stirring a venture to back out. Without detail, prior to Lynn and Marlo's arrival, I gave Marlo a cursory account of recent spirit experiences in my home. This would be her first visit and I was interested in her insight.

When the women arrived, Marlo quietly took in the energy as we walked alongside the wall in my living room. On the other side was a closet in my oldest son's room. Stopping, Marlo said the atmosphere had changed. It was colder in this particular spot. She said this was where the energies were coming from. She didn't know that my younger son had recently told me he felt there was a vortex, a spiritual passageway, in his brother's closet. It provided the spirits an entry into our home. Confirmations were starting. It was time to begin.

I unfolded a new card table, placing three chairs at it. At Marlo's instruction, we burned sage and cedar to cleanse the atmosphere and our own auras. We poured a circle of salt around us for protection from negative energies. I sat with Lynn, an old acquaintance, and Marlo, a new acquaintance, and accepted both in their respective roles in our endeavor. Having had the most spiritual encounters, without debate, Marlo was the most qualified to take the lead. Lynn was the designated watcher. She had participated in a séance or two prior to this night and if anything should go awry, if I should become entangled in becoming the object of any spirit's quest, I trusted that Lynn would do whatever was necessary to extract me. Calming my fears, I took a deep breath, preparing myself for what was to come. I let go of any apprehensions that might inhibit connecting to the other side. I had to take part at full capacity. I could not be afraid.

Anticipating an experience that would bring me closer to understanding the finer points of life and death, I was ready. To document this moment, I turned on a newly purchased tape recorder, bought just for this occasion. I wanted to have all bases covered. I would have my notes afterwards but I needed something to seize the sounds and other details I may not remember or be aware of during the session.

Carefully selected, this instrument was certain to perform exceptionally well, maintaining the integrity of the manufacturer. Testing it prior to the occasion, it clearly recorded sounds coming from one floor above. It was perfect for this turning point in my spiritual growth. With a brand new tape cassette, I placed the machine about three feet away, just outside of my reach. It was far enough to be out of the way, yet close enough to pick up any and every sound or vibration. If it could record happenings from upstairs, through the floor, I was sure there would be no issues with it in the same room.

Sitting, we took deep breaths in unison and closed our eyes to Marlo's directives. Slowly counting to eight, my spirit flowed gently with the numbers. It was quite relaxing. Besides the three of us, there was no one else in my home. With everyone seated, Marlo began some sort of invocation, calling on the positive forces around us. In these last moments before our ascent, I hoped I would not go into a trance. I wanted to remain conscious of my surroundings and my reactions. How else could I say, beyond any doubt, that this was real? It was time. I let go of all thoughts.

Within seconds, my jaw dropped and locked. My mouth was wide open. It was not of my doing and I was amazed. I had no control over what was happening and did not fight it. I could feel this was not a negative force and found myself allowing the energy to prove its existence to me, through me. I remained calm so that I could fully experience this phenomenon. Truthfully, I didn't know how all of this worked. Though I had accepted the energy that had arrived, if it should manifest itself into physical form, the greater part of me did not want to see it. So, I closed my eyes.

I rhythmically drummed on the table with my hands. Lynn and Marlo, sitting on either side of me, held my wrists down. I started laughing, saying in a singsong sort of way, *Bee Bop! Bee Bop!* Answering questions from Lynn and Marlo, I described myself as a rotund, brown-skinned man, sporting a goatee and mustache, wearing a black tam. I was in France, at a small corner café, with cobblestone streets and fresh air. I loved this area. I felt very much at home. When Lynn asked who I was, I called out a name: *Dizzy!* Then, at the thought of a particular woman, I dropped my head into silence. There was a deep sadness. She was a true love, a lost love. As quickly as he came, he was gone.

Marlo, sitting to my right, was now speaking, calling on evil spirits. With eyes closed, I turned her way, wondering what she was doing. We had agreed this would be a positive experience but she was now calling on negative forces. The moment I heard her utter the word *Satan* I reacted. *No!* I began moving my arms. Wielding a sword in either hand, I made precise, well-executed martial arts movements against this enemy. It was now spirit-to-spirit. The sounds coming from my mouth were those of a samurai warrior, intent on stopping his opponent. Lynn asked this spirit its name. Without hesitation, in a deep, powerful voice I bellowed, *I am the Protector!* I was Samurai. Marlo's character shrunk back and disappeared, and we resumed.

Other, less forceful, spirits came through and within an hour, we were done. To preserve the experience, on a piece of paper, we quickly jotted down the names of the forces we had experienced: Dizzy, Cab, the Samurai, Satan, Jean, the little girl in the grave, the little boy with his little sister. The three of us signed it.

Marlo was spiritually drained and left with Lynn almost immediately afterwards. With much to think about, it was time to listen to the evening's activity. I was certain, on my recorder, there were things we may not have heard or remembered. I wanted to hear what my voice sounded like as these spirits manifested through me. I was curious about this Samurai, Japan's most courageous of warriors, protectors of the land. I wondered if my tone was different. Did I take on an accent? Was it one of my ancestors? I had many questions and listened eagerly.

I moved the tape forward and forward some more. I pushed the rewind button. I turned up the volume. There was nothing. I checked my recorder with another tape, which worked fine, and listened again. There was only the sound of hissing, empty air. What happened? Consulting Marlo the next day, she gave a simple answer: the spirits did not want any recording. Well… okay.

Though it appeared there would be nothing to corroborate our séance, I refused to give up. In the days that followed, I listened to the tape for Marlo's introduction, for Lynn's words, and for my own voice. There seemed to be no validation that this séance took place. But I knew these sounds existed because I was physically present. Not only had I heard the words, I had spoken some of them. But my own resounding voice was non-detectable and I couldn't hear Lynn or Marlo. None of our voices registered. How was this possible?

Discouraged over my lack of proof, I continued listening, gauging the moment I would submit and wave the surrender flag. If there was nothing in the first few minutes, the chances of hearing anything at all was slim. I heard whispers, mumblings and mutterings, but could not determine the words said or which of us was saying them. Just as I was about to give up, at fifteen minutes and eleven seconds in, I heard what sounded like two large knives clanking together, as though someone was sharpening them. When did that happen? I quickly scanned my memory. The samurai! This was when he wielded his swords against the evil force of Satan. I was elated. This was something concrete. It wasn't much but it existed. And not that anyone else would know what this sound was. But I knew.

Soon afterwards, I began seeing the samurai, in my mind's eye. He was always dressed in his black and red formal attire, his suit of armor, horned helmet, and sword. His self-proclaimed duty was to protect my home. He would pace my front yard or sit on the front steps. It was interesting to me that he never went into the backyard where the dogs were. After seeing him a few times, I mentioned this to my youngest son. He said he could see him also. Without divulging any detailed information, I asked him to describe our new guardian. He did. Perfectly.

This particular year, I invited Marlo and Lynn to my home for Thanksgiving dinner. As I sat at my kitchen counter speaking with Marlo, I saw her face transform. I can only describe it as being in front of those mirrors in a fun house, the ones that distort your reflection into an elongated, squiggly mass. It lasted only a moment, but it was a big moment for me. I was incredulous. I consumed no drugs or alcohol so this could not have been a hallucination. Of course, I mentioned this to Marlo and was even more stunned at her calm reception. Did that mean this had happened before?

Marlo believed in the possibility that we evolved from aliens so my revelation wasn't a far-off thought to her. I, however, had never thought about it. And I'm still not sure I can believe it. I do know, however, what I saw.

~ A SECOND SÉANCE ~

Disappointed at not having a full recording of the first séance, I participated in a second. This time, on December 01, 2003, a Monday, my youngest son joined Lynn, Marlo, and myself. Once again, we cleansed the air with sage and scattered salt for our protection. Once again, I used a tape recorder. We relaxed, closed our eyes, and began our ascent.

I connected with a young girl, about six years old, on a riverbank. There had been a car accident. To the left, there was a grey stone bridge with water running underneath. Scared, the little girl was crying. Her older sister was trying to coax her across the bridge, to be with her but she was too frightened to move. She did not understand why her sister would not come get her. She did not know where their mother was and she wanted to be with her. I felt distressed. I cried aloud in her place, with the voice of a six year old.

The pieces of this puzzle began unfolding. This little girl was dead. So was her sister, who was trying to persuade her to cross over the bridge, to make her transition. Without her mother, however, the girl was too afraid. She was afraid to be without her family and confused at her death. As the little girl's conduit, I knew I had to convince her it was okay to cross the bridge. After several pleadings, the little girl was finally convinced that her mother and sister had themselves transitioned over and were waiting for her on the other side. To be with them, the little girl crossed over. She made a fine transition, connecting with her family.

Without lapse, one spiritual scene led into another. My son was talking. *No! Johnny, put the knife down. Take care of your brother.* It was brief. Only after our session did I understand what the words meant. My son had served as conduit for my paternal grandmother, someone who had died long before he was born. And there was quite a bit of family trivia he did not know. He didn't know that the family referred to my father by the name, Johnny, instead of a more formal John. He did not know that since his boyhood in the Bronx until his death in 1995, my father carried a knife for personal protection: *No! Johnny, put the knife down*. Or that he was fiercely protective of his family: *Take care of your brother.*

In 1967, my father's older brother, Earl, had died during an unprovoked knife attack by a transient in New York City. My uncle's murder devastated my father who felt, in some way, he should have been there to protect him. I was convinced this revelation was from my grandmother to my father, regarding my uncle. It seems they were together now in the spirit realm.

The information was appearing quickly. There was a little girl in the woods. She was crying. It was an assault. It was Leonard. *Get Leonard!*

Instantly transported to a beautiful expanse in Wyoming, it was a striking picture of greenery, of nature's glory. I accepted the life of a young Native American male, going by the name of Youngblood. In his early thirties, he was dressed in casual American garb, a light-blue, long sleeved shirt to be exact. The man was in the throes of deep sorrow, sobbing in anguish. Our heads (his and mine) tilted back to the heavens and we cried out, *Father! Father! They have taken my son!* His words came from the most intense part of our souls. I could feel the agony as if it were my own. His guttural howl was drenched in pain as we continued his cry, *Father! Help me!*

The white men had come and had taken the man's child. Not knowing what to do, he sought guidance and solace from his deceased father, an elder of their tribe. In these seconds, Youngblood and I were separate and, at the same time, we were one. As he wept, I wept, my spirit saturated with a sense of hollowness. Youngblood's father was stern, but loving. He instructed him to not seek revenge... *the gods will bring justice.*

I opened my eyes. In the midst of our grief, tears had formed, ready to escape down onto my face. This was real. It is difficult to corral the words to describe the emotions of this scene. It was spiritually demanding, feeling this kind of pain. As I remember this experience for this book, I feel an emotional heaviness that still catches in my heart.

This session was also tape recorded, also with little audio results. I have since learned of particular audio equipment that can be used to capture spirit sounds. I am not certain of the accuracy of the information spoken during either of these séances. All I can tell you, with absolute certainty, is that we received it. Marlo has since made her transition. Rest in peace.

~ SPIRIT GUIDES ~

Are there truly angels and spirit guides to help smooth the sometimes-rough terrain of our existence? After becoming acquainted with various aspects of the supernatural world, I had become unconvinced that everyone had a spirit guide. I had been politely listening to others' talk of having developed personal relationships with their very own spirit guides, even coming to know them by name. They communicated with them on a regular basis and chattered on about how everyone had *at least one*. I wasn't a believer. While I did not doubt their experiences. I didn't really believe them either. After all, where were *my* guides, *my* protectors? Sure, several years ago, there was my grandfather. And there was the samurai who sat by the door for a short while. But who was sitting on my shoulder, watching and guiding me? I decided to consult a psychic reader to answer this question.

I had found a fabulous place in Roswell, Georgia that smelled of incense and mysticism and had in-house psychics. I had been there on other occasions and this time, in June 2007, I was there to see Errin. A young, spirited person, I hoped he would have the answers I needed. After introductions, I set my tape recorder (which I have referred to for this entry) and we began our session.

Errin described himself as a channeler. Spirits utilized him as a conduit, to relay messages. His intuitive aspects are sight, smell, and touch.

Closing his eyes, he allowed his connection to begin. His words flowed cryptically...

> *... it is our intention... at this time that... this reading... in its entirety... in this environment be done... through source, for source, by source, for... the highest good of... all souls involved.*

Soon after we began, Errin said there were numerous energies vying for his attention. Thinking I was only interested in my spirit guides, I got an immediate response. Errin said, since childhood, I have had several guides with me. *Really.* Despite my recent experiences, I was still a spiritual skeptic. Oh yeah, he said, they had talked to me all the time. I wasn't impressed. It sounded rather cliché, general information that could have applied to anyone. Alarms sounded in my head, *Fake! Fake!* Most importantly, I had no recollection of it.

Nevertheless, I owed it to myself to think about it. After all, this was a paid session. I should cooperate. I quickly scanned my mind of almost fifty years. Nothing. Not one incident. After years of working in law enforcement, and more years growing up in New Jersey, it was difficult to accept this information without proof. Errin would have to do better. I needed specifics.

Just as I dismissed Errin's words, my mind flashed back to when I was three and four years old. My imaginary friends. The memory was now very clear. It was something I had long forgotten. Transported back to my bedroom, in pre-kindergarten wonderment, I sat on the floor, laughing and playing. These adult people were especially nice and reserved. I see that they didn't sit cross-legged on the floor the way I did. They knelt on their knees and sat back on their calves and heels of their feet. Were they part of my Asian heritage? For the first time, I absorbed those moments. I accepted them. Now, I was certain. They were not my imagination after all. They were a real spiritual experience.

~ REVELATIONS and PREMONITIONS ~

Cold readings are impromptu. There is no time to alter the information or influence it with my own opinions. I don't dictate whose past, present, or future I will see or which part of anyone's life becomes available to me. It happens naturally.

- *Revelation: an act of revealing, or making known.*

- *Premonition: implies warning, or notice of an imminent danger or occurrence.*

Adrienne

September 2004. I had known Adrienne for many years and while we were on friendly terms, I knew little of her personal life and vice versa. She did not know of my ability to perceive and I did not know if she was a believer. As we spoke, I ignored the visions that began appearing in my mind, as a sidebar to Adrienne's voice. I saw her in places I never knew she had been, standing inside a crowded subway train. There was a man behind her, to her right, wearing a military uniform. The words were specific: *army green*. She was susceptible to the energy of the other passengers and it made her uncomfortable.

Snubbing my visions didn't make them less intrusive. The energy urging me to share them with Adrienne wouldn't go away. It was best that I present the information to her, rather than ignore it. How do I share it in a way that would seem less insane?

I started with an ordinary question, asking Adrienne how often she rode the subway trains. I was surprised at her curt and icy response, her change in demeanor. She went from friendly and talkative to tight-lipped and formal. She said she had never been on the trains and that she hated them. Okay. I had to accept it. After all, who was I to say she had done something she hadn't? Maybe I was wrong. We talked another five or ten minutes and though I had begun to doubt myself, the images continued. Unable to disregard them, I asked Adrienne if she was sure she had never been on a subway train and described in detail what I was seeing.

My images were clear and, it turned out, also accurate. This time Adrienne shared that while on a recent job assignment in New York City, she rode the subway train for the first time. As you can guess, it was crowded, packed tight with multitudes of energies flickering about. She began to sense negative energy from others around her and became frightened. She decided never to ride the subway again. Her companion was a military man. Now, I understood the reference to the army green color.

We went on to talk for hours, discussing the images strolling my mind. I saw the troubles she was having at her workplace. I accurately described the offender and the seriousness of his behavior. I also saw her connection to the supernatural. Adrienne confirmed the information and said that on a recent jaunt to New Orleans, she had wandered from her intended path into a shop of potions, spells, and supernatural paraphernalia. She felt an uneasy connection and when the attendant urged her into a back room, she and her companion promptly left.

Adrienne also shared a family experience from years prior, when her mother had seen the spirit of a little boy in their home. She did a spiritual cleansing and, through prayer, expelled the energy. They later found that the spirit had moved next door. It was now pestering a neighbor.

Trisha

Not only was I communicating with others who had an understanding, an interest, or aptitude in the metaphysical aspect of life, I was steadily displaying an ability to see. Trisha was a psychic I had met through a mutual acquaintance. One day, I began having images of Trisha embroiled in a situation. I could clearly see her in a courtroom setting, in a highly irrational state. Though I did not know why she was in court, I was in the moment with her. I felt her emotional breakdown and knew it would cause the judge to rule against her. I shared my vision with her and received acknowledgment that she was in the midst of a custody battle. I advised her to be calm in her presentation, as this was the only way to create a favorable outcome. If she were to become emotionally unhinged, she would lose. Following my instructions, the case fell in her favor.

Salina and Terri

I had known Salina and her family for several years. Her seventeen-year-old daughter, Terri, had recently married and relocated to another state. It was a volatile relationship and Salina hadn't heard from Terri in quite some time. She was naturally concerned and expressed a possibility that Terri might not be alive.

While Salina spoke, in my mind's eye, I saw an arid area, a lone leafless tree, and dried brush. I saw no death. According to the information I was receiving, Terri was alive but was *in the middle of nowhere*. Salina tried to get me to confirm or deny her worst fear, but I would not. Any situation regarding the well-being of a son or daughter is a delicate one. I wasn't so confident in my abilities to relay the knowledge, one way or the other. What would the emotional ramifications be if I said Terri was okay but she wasn't? Or that she wasn't okay, and she was. I considered myself a novice with this psychic ability thing and did not want to be the messenger. But the information continued. *She will contact a relative.*

No one knew where Terri was but I knew she would be contacting someone. Whether physically or by spirit, Terri would communicate. I relayed the information to Salina, who said that Terri had a favorite aunt. If she communicated with anyone, it would be her. I encouraged Salina to direct her prayers towards that. Shortly afterwards, I got word that Terri had communicated with this aunt by telephone. She was safe. Out driving with her husband, they had squabbled and he, with a young and fragile ego, had ordered her out of the car. *In the middle of nowhere.*

Derwin

In 2000, after fourteen years of working in law enforcement, I was considering retirement. The apathy was affecting me and I felt a need to be in a different environment. Derwin Brown, a captain in my police department, and one of my first police academy instructors, had won his bid to become sheriff of our county. I applied for a position and, in early December, received notice that I had a new job, beginning in January 2001.

My pending transfer was bittersweet. I reminisced on the past fourteen years and contemplated my future. Without regretting my decision in joining the police force, I looked forward to a new start. I was content at the thought of working alongside a man who lived to make positive change. But as the days inched along, an unsettling feeling came over me. *You're not going over* were the words that played in my head. It made me uneasy. It made me doubtful. It created a sense of gloom. What had changed?

I called Alicia, an academy-mate, for consolation and confirmation. Also transferring from the police department to the sheriff's office, she was a close friend to Derwin. If my new position with the sheriff's office were in jeopardy, she would have the inside scoop. Though she said everything was good, that nothing had changed, the words nagged my mind... *you're not going over*.

It was a Friday evening, December 15, 2000. I was at home, lying on my couch, pondering my new beginning. The telephone rang. It was Alicia. She got straight to the point. *They shot him*, she said. What? Ambushed in the driveway of his home as he returned from his victory celebration dinner, Derwin was now in the emergency room of the local medical center. He would not survive his wounds.

Derwin's murder was heart wrenching. All involved with this crime were from law enforcement backgrounds. The former sheriff included. I was devastated. That night, on a fundamental level, my view on law enforcement changed forever. I would never overcome the knowledge that another law enforcement officer would commit this heinous act of violence, particularly against one of his own brethren. And, just as those words indicated, I was not going over. There was no transfer.

Denise and Mr. M

February 2005. Denise was receiving frequent phone calls from her elderly father, who was living on his own, in another state. It was unusual for him to call so often and she was concerned. Through the years, Denise had wanted to come to some kind of a decision as to what she could do to help care for him. As with most elders, Mr. M was comfortable in his own home and would not consider moving. Nor would he agree to travel, even for a short stay with his daughter.

Talking with Denise, the energy was strong. I knew she had to get to her father, to check on his wellness. I told her so and she immediately made flight arrangements. I received a phone call from her shortly after her arrival. Her father had not been properly taking his medication. With no one assisting him on a consistent basis to administer his prescriptions, it had created medical issues. She had reached him in time to help.

To Denise's surprise, without fuss, her father agreed to visit with her for a short while. The words that came to me were clear and concise: *he won't be back*. Mr. M would not be returning to his home. Passing along this bit of information, just as I had received it, I could hear Denise take in a breath. But she said nothing.

A day or so later, Denise revealed that she had arrived to her father's home to find he had begun packing his bags. He had given away furniture and other personal property to family and friends, preparing to make a permanent move with her, to her home. It was a good and timely decision. Hospitalized briefly within a week of his move, with Denise's care, Mr. M recovered and lived until his transition in 2014. Rest in peace Mr. M.

Imani

Imani's birthday luncheon was a happy gathering of friends and associates. Though everyone, with the exception of Imani, was a stranger to me, there was spirit bonding. As I engaged in conversation with one guest, I immediately saw images of a man and then, a snake. I reactively threw up my right hand, with my middle and index fingers posing as fangs. The guest gasped. She had been having difficulty understanding the energy of a particular man she knew, someone who held a trustworthy position in her community. She felt he had the nature of a snake, that he could not be trusted. Today her thoughts were confirmed.

Olivia and Demetri

Sometimes my visions and premonitions take time to come to fruition. In January 2005, I had spoken with Olivia by telephone. Her son, Demetri, was friends with my youngest son. We talked about their current events and I learned that Demetri was planning to relocate to another state. As I listened, I began receiving knowledge. The words were that *he has to stop being a certain way*. It alluded to Demetri's alcohol consumption.

Uncertain how Olivia would accept this personal information, I didn't pass it on as straightforward as I had received it. I was specific, yet discreet. If she knew of his activities, she would understand my words. She did. The number 26 also came to my mind, though Olivia could not associate it with Demetri's move.

On June 10, 2007, Demetri died in a vehicle accident. His car capsized and he was unable to release himself from his seatbelt. He drowned in just a few feet of water. There was evidence of alcohol use, which contributed to his inability to extricate himself. On his upcoming birthday, in September, he would have been 26 years old.

My heart ached for Demetri. And for Olivia. I had an emotional meltdown, thinking about the delicacy of life. Though I understood that no one has control over anyone else's destiny, I wondered if there was something, anything, I could have done to redirect this circumstance. Was there something more I should have seen?

On June 2, 2007, just eight days prior, my oldest son had been in a car accident. Visiting for the weekend, he had borrowed my car for the evening and, on the way back to my home, had fallen asleep at the wheel. His only memory of the event was regaining consciousness and thinking that no one would find him in the dark. He drove to a well-lit area (a nearby gas station that had closed for the night) and lost consciousness again. A passerby saw him and called 911. He thought my son was dead.

Fortunately, my son escaped with only a few scrapes and bruises. My mangled car did not survive. The tires were shredded and the rims bent. The roof had caved in and the trunk lid was missing. The only area without damage was a rear quarter panel, where the gas tank was. Because of its condition, the responding officer said no one could have driven it and insisted it had been towed to this current location. A diligent second officer continued searching until she located the accident site, just two blocks away. My trunk lid was lying on a nearby lawn with contents from my car strewn across it. The evidence formed the story that my car had plummeted down a short embankment, did a 180-degree turn, and traveled backwards through trees before stopping. Had it continued facing forward, the engine would have likely ended in my son's lap. Instead, the rear of the car absorbed the impact.

What was mystical about this incident was that my son always drove his car on his trips home. This time he rode with a friend. Had he been in his own vehicle, there could well have been a different outcome. And my car, heavier and sturdier, was a replacement for one I had lost in an accident years prior. Purchased with my expressed concern for the safety of my family, I now wondered if it was a premonition coming to fruition, five years later. And then, was there a force with my son, guiding him out of the darkness, to an area where he would be found and helped?

Brenda and Jasmine

In 2009, Jasmine had disappeared from her family home. She was a rebel, a runaway, a young person just into her teens. Like many youngsters during this stage, she thought she could do better on her own. Of course, her mother, Brenda, was concerned. Speaking with her, I received the words that Jasmine was *across town*. I saw her walking through a parking lot, walking away from wherever she was. I didn't know this place but I relayed the information as I received it.

Jasmine returned home shortly afterwards, alive and well. According to Brenda, she had been a couple of cities over from where they lived. She had been *across town*. Out walking with a group of youngsters going to a nearby convenience store, Jasmine decided to go home. She casually walked through the parking lot and began the long walk home.

Pearl

Pearl, still a dear friend, recently reminded me of two experiences. While driving with her through her neighborhood a few years ago, in my mind's eye, I saw a young Native American man. He was running through the wooded area we were passing, chased by someone, or something, not visible to me. Of course, given the history of our nation, this was possible. There are spirits everywhere.

The second incident was a bruise on Pearl's arm. She didn't know how she had gotten it. It appeared the night before but there was no pain. Not knowing it was there, she could not pinpoint how it happened. Had it not been on this highly visible area of her body, she may not have noticed it at all. I had a sudden urge to reach out, to heal this bruise, by rubbing it. The image in my mind, from my third eye, was not my finger reaching out. It was a longer digit, similar to the renowned ET, the extraterrestrial. I know. This does sound outlandish, doesn't it? It sounds as if I am not stable but I assure you, I am.

I resisted this spiritual impulse. On two separate occasions, in small gatherings of people, I had been mysteriously compelled to reach out and touch others. Literally. I was mortified. Reserved by nature, it was disturbing to me and, I'm sure, invasive for them. I could see what I was doing but taken by surprise, I felt not in control. It seemed that some other force was using me to resolve its own curiosity. It had been embarrassing and I was now making every effort to be in control of this behavior. I was not going to touch Pearl's arm. Even if it was to help.

Until the image vanished from my mind, I instructed Pearl to rub the bruise on her arm. And she did. Two days later, I received a phone call from her. The bruise had disappeared. Strangely, it didn't go through the usual healing process. There was no gradual fading from the dark color to the lighter tones. It was… just… gone.

Joe

In 1987, at the start of my law enforcement career, Joe and I were in the same academy. In 2007, we were working together in the office of the Chief of Police. One day, out running errands, we had an easy conversation that led to talk of spirituality. I shared with him my ability to *see* and without question or pause, he asked about a promotion he had been promised. It was something he sincerely wanted but it hadn't transpired thus far. Joe was becoming discouraged.

Many officers envision themselves in supervisory positions, so Joe's aspiration wasn't unusual. A promotion signified accomplishment and boosts pension benefits at retirement. But, as Joe spoke, I heard an emphatic *No!* It was in my inner ear and it was clear. There was no doubt there would not be any rank advancement. At least, not under the current administration.

I knew that this information could crush Joe's spirit. Being mindful of that, and any destruction my revelation could cause, I battled within myself. Should I be truthful, or should I not? How should I disclose this information? Dismayed at the predicament I was in, I had only seconds to decide. I had to make a choice. I took in a breath and told Joe he would get his promotion. Yes. I lied.

Joe was elated. I was not. I knew that my dishonesty was injurious to my credibility and my credibility has always been vital to me. Most important though, at that moment, was that I did not want to be the cause of any dissension between Joe and the superior that promised him the promotion. Shortly afterwards, there was a swift rearranging of personnel. Joe was reassigned to another detail and, as was the prediction, he never made rank under this management.

Work Related

Though the law enforcement environment was generally not conducive to connecting to spirits and energies, on a few occasions I received information on a particular case I was working on.

A woman reported the forgery of her personal check and suspected her daughter. Moving forward in the investigation, she came in to the precinct to give a written statement. As she spoke, I saw a male figure connected to the incident. The word *underground* came to me, along with the image of a bus stop near a bank. In reviewing the details of this case, the victim revealed that she believed her daughter's boyfriend was also involved. A subsequent photo of the transaction placed him at a bank in Atlanta, Georgia, negotiating the check. It was near a bus stop, across the street from an underground area of shops and eateries aptly named The Underground.

On another occasion, while in a bank working on a fraud case, a woman approached me. "Detective", she said. "Do you remember me?" I didn't. Sometimes, in the moment of trying to help someone, all that matters is that you help. Faces and details may become obscure. I didn't remember but I began getting images of a young man wearing a military uniform and a younger sister. I had never had an encounter with any young man in a military uniform while working any of my cases. What did this brother and sister have to do with this woman?

As the image flowed, I turned my attention back to the woman who was simultaneously saying that, after my meeting with her son, he had made a personal transformation. From being on a road leading nowhere good, he was now in the U.S. Army, doing well. The woman had a daughter, the young man's little sister, was so very proud of him.

Stan

2007. Stan was a musician leading a jet-set kind of life. We had never traveled in the same social circles but when the age difference between us became less loud, we connected. There was an immediate spirit attachment, something I could not reasonably explain. There were images and words and as the knowledge filtered in, I learned we had shared previous lifetimes. Two, to be exact. One, as brother and sister, the other, a doomed, wrong-timing kind of romantic relationship. This current lifetime was an emotional culmination of those existences.

Without any direct contact, I could see Stan as a child of five or six years old, wearing short pants and a jacket with no lapels. This image of him as a boy was long before I knew of him and years before I was born. I received knowledge about his career, of his karmic blocks, of his spirit. He was quite astonished, given we had just recently met. None of it was common knowledge and some of it was his own personal reflections. I couldn't have heard it from anyone.

One message for Stan was a warning. Sitting together one evening, the words were clear and crisp. I knew little of Stan's personal life but in these brief moments, I could feel the weight of his overall health. *You should get more rest* were the words that came to me. Though prompted to pass them along, since we were not close friends, I was cautious of intruding on his personal space. After some minutes and continual spiritual nudging, I delivered the missive as respectfully as I could. I did not have specifics and hoped he could accept it, just as it was. Without looking up, his response was that he had much to do, leaving little time to rest. While he didn't say so, it seemed he had accepted that proper repose was near impossible.

The topic of Stan's health seemed significant and I continued thinking about it afterwards. Uncertain how he would absorb additional information, I relayed them primarily through email correspondence.

I made mention of you getting proper rest. I didn't tell you, but the words that you were wearing yourself out and you could well shorten your life were very plain. Please take extra good care of yourself.

Stan acknowledged the message and I later revealed to him our life as brother and sister. I explained that, in a previous lifetime, I had been his dedicated older sibling. *Devoted* was the word I had received. I had watched over him with a deep sense of responsibility for his care, as if he were my own child. This emotion transcended time, remaining strong lifetime after lifetime and clarified the concern I felt for him currently. About a year and a half later, Stan had a major health upset. It was serious. Hospitalized, fatigue was a factor in his declining health.

Rahn

Rahn lives in a home surrounded by trees and greenery. I have known him for almost three decades and we often have conversations regarding spirituality. This day, outside of his home, having our usual talk, I had a flash of him jogging naked into the woods. It was not a sexual image. It was a spiritual one. There were no details of his anatomy, just his body flowing into the woods. I mentioned this to Rahn without hesitation. He smiled and told me that when the mood strikes him, he will walk through his property, into the woods... naked.

Kym and Kyle

Kym believes in spiritual guidance and receives information via her dreams. We don't talk often but when we do, spiritualism is usually a topic for review.

Colors are significant in my association with Kym. During one conversation, as she spoke about her deceased mother, the colors pink and green were dominant. I never knew Kym's mother and thought it a peculiar combination. I thought, maybe, they were favorite colors. Flashing in my mind several more times, I had to ask Kym about the connection. Her answer was that pink and green are the colors of the sorority her mother pledged.

On another occasion, I saw Kym's father (also deceased) standing, dressed in the color brown. From head to toe, he wore a brown shirt, brown pants, and a brown hat. It was a perfect blend. When I mentioned this, Kym shrieked, *"That's my father's favorite color!"* He even drove a brown car.

On October 24, 2016, Kym's son, Kyle, made his transition. 30-ish, he was her only child. I listened as Kym reminisced and laughed at the memories her son had given her. An image came to my mind of Kyle sitting, dressed in white, with a brilliant shade of red around him. I knew Kyle, but did not know any intimate details of his life. I asked Kym how he was associated with this color, red. Quietly, she said it was his favorite.

Kym and Kyle had a close mother/son relationship. To help her maintain a positive perspective Kym said that though Kyle had passed on physically, she knew he would always be with her in spirit. More than that, I told her. He was with her now. He had shown me his favorite color so she would know this message was from him, for her.

He said, *Ma! I'm never gonna leave you.* For Kym, during this time, it was the next best thing to a hug.

On December 1, 2016, Kym and I spoke. She shared that every day was a different day in overcoming the loss of her son. We talked. First about incidental topics and then about Kyle. The same as the day he died, Kyle was adamant about being with his mother. I could see him. I could feel him. But in a swift change of emotion, I could see that he was angry with his mother today. I told this to Kym.

Kym has always been receptive to any knowledge I have to pass along to her. She is always open to receiving messages. Today, her son was disturbed about something she had done, something she was doing. *I don't want you here with me* are the words I received. The implication was that Kyle did not want Kym to join him in death. I didn't understand but I relayed the information. Kym sighed. She said this was her worst day since Kyle's death. Earlier in the day, she was out walking and crying. Heartbroken, she missed her son deeply. She had thought about what it would take to be with him.

It was clear that Kyle's spirit was with Kym. He clearly wanted her to know that his dimension was not where she should be. He wanted her to live. Kym embraced the message and gathered her strength. We talked more. I heard the word *butter*. How unusual. Was this Kyle's favorite topping on some food? Maybe rice? Kym roared with laughter. No, it was something else. Something too personal to include here, but it was real. Kym knew. This was a good reading. It created happiness and hope. Be peaceful Kym. Rest in peace Kyle.

Sue

In support of a mutual friend on her journey as a spiritual advisor, Sue and I went to Tanesha's debut at a psychic fair. On our return drive, I listened as Sue spoke about her family, particularly her father. As she spoke, I could see the maroon color spattered about and the word *everywhere* came to my mind. I ignored the vision until it dominated my thoughts and I finally had to mention it. Sue informed me that the recognizing color for her father's high school was maroon. In fact, at some point in their lives, most of her family had attended this school. Hence, the maroon color *everywhere*.

Ananda

2016. I spoke with Ananda by telephone. Spiritually searching, she was just beginning to study the Wiccan life. She was becoming comfortable in accepting her role as a clairvoyant and wanted to fulfill her purpose.

Ananda revealed that her great-grandmother and grandfather, both deceased, often visit her. I could see them connecting with her and described her great-grandmother's quiet nature along with her ferocity in protecting her. Ananda confirmed this information.

Her grandfather's spirit came through and I could feel that though he carried the burdens of his life's struggles, he maintained a light-hearted, jovial spirit. I could also see a plaid pattern related to him. Ananda laughed and said he always wore plaid shirts. I mentioned that it was important that she knew that her grandfather wanted her to *let go of being sad*. I didn't know what it pertained to but I relayed the information. Ananda shared that she felt regret and sadness that, deployed to the Middle East she was unable to attend her grandfather's funeral. He didn't want her to fret over this and said, *Baby, don't worry. I understand*. The message lifted Ananda's spirit.

~ PAST LIFE REGRESSION ~

January 2017. Rondell had been one of my youngest son's closest friends and had transitioned thirteen years earlier, at the young age of twenty years old. He was a spirit who had absorbed life with an urgency. His mother, Cecilia, shared that, from an early age, he could foresee he would not live a long life. An illness brought that prediction to fruition.

Cecilia moved from the area and, years later, when she returned, I welcomed her into my home. Though we had been aware of one another's existence so many years ago, this was our first time sharing space, breaking bread. It was an unexpected spiritual encounter.

During the course of our conversation, Cecilia and I discovered our commonality in spirituality and psychic ability, and made a natural progression into a previous lifetime. We discovered that, at one time, I had been an Egyptian ruler and Cecilia, my spiritual healer. I was also able to identify a family member with me during that time, putting into place our current connection, presenting me with a better understanding of our present bond.

When our journey was complete, Cecilia shared that when she had entered my home her spirit had referenced me being a male. Not wanting to insult me, she said nothing. Now, we were able to understand the information and that it was a prelude to our visit to the remote past.

With Rondell our common denominator, we all felt his energy. I described certain characteristics his spirit exhibited this evening, such as resting his head on my shoulder while I touched his long hair. Cecilia confirmed it as a favorite pastime she had shared with her son. She said he loved to rest his head on her shoulder while she gently touched his hair. Rest in peace Rondell.

~ FINAL FAREWELLS... *maybe* ~

Mrs. Ellis had made her transition about a year and a half ago. On March 5, 2017, at her spiritual behest, I went to visit her home. She wanted to say goodbye to this place she and her family had called home for almost three decades. It had, indeed, been a sanctuary for them and their many friends.

Daughter Pearl met me at the door. Usually brimming with energy, the house was quiet now. The television wasn't blurting the news and there were no groups of people engaged in philosophical dialogue. It was quiet and still.

Soon after my arrival, Mrs. Ellis, in spirit, made herself known to me. As an aside, it's interesting to me that spirits often appear to us as their recognizable human selves rather than unrecognizable balls of energy. I suppose it makes it more palatable to digest and easier to connect if we can identify with whatever has appeared. And I wonder if recognition of the spiritual presence is the manifestation of the spirit's will or our perception of it. In any case, I digress. Mrs. Ellis was present.

Sitting in the kitchen, I was prompted to get up from my seat and walk to a patio door. Looking out, I felt peaceful. Mrs. Ellis' energy felt peaceful. Pearl said that her mother loved to stand there and watch for the cardinals that would fly into the yard. They were a sign of good fortune. After sitting back down and resuming our dialogue, I was again impelled to get up. Mrs. Ellis wanted to lead me. I told Pearl to follow.

I walked where Mrs. Ellis walked. Through the living room, stopping for a quick prayer. To the left, to a part of the home I had never been. I kept my head down, eyes looking towards the floor, so that I could not see where we were headed. I didn't want to unconsciously influence our destination. Turn right? No. Left. Watching my steps, we walked down a carpeted hall. I could see we were at a doorway.

Stepping in, and now looking up, it was a bedroom. It was still. Peaceful. I asked Pearl whose bedroom this was. It was her parents' room.

We sat for a quick prayer and Mrs. Ellis got my attention. She was moving to the right. There were several pictures on top of a dresser but only one stood out. True, it was the largest, but it was the only one Mrs. Ellis acknowledged. It was the one that she loved. And Pearl confirmed this. It was Mrs. Ellis' favorite photo of her husband in his younger years. Now, she was ready to leave.

Several weeks later, while visiting Pearl with mutual friends, we sat down for evening prayer. There was more than enough seating and I chose a random chair to sit in, placing my handbag on a stool. At the start of our prayer, I felt Mrs. Ellis' spirit. A feeling washed over me, telling me to move my handbag to another seat. It wasn't an order or command. Mrs. Ellis was not the demanding type. It was a suggestion. One I resisted. I saw nothing wrong with where my bag was. When Mrs. Ellis would not move on, I moved it. But it wasn't enough. Now, the proposition was that I sit in another chair. I sat firm. Surely, Mrs. Ellis would leave me alone. She didn't. I acknowledged her spirit. I bowed. And I moved.

Afterwards, I told Pearl about this incident. She told me that she had noticed my moment of playing musical chairs and said the chair I moved from was Mrs. Ellis' favorite when she prayed.

Mrs. Bailey

In her late eighties, Mrs. Bailey was quiet but courageous. And deeply sincere. Though our contact could be considered miniscule, in Mrs. Bailey's presence, I always felt that she understood my soul. And she respected it. It was a tacit embrace of my existence, of my fundamental being. Though I had intended to visit her and her family over the years, it never came to pass. And then, she was gone.

In January 2017, when Mrs. Bailey made her transition, I naturally offered prayers for her eternal light. In turn, she spoke to me. In February, I journeyed to Chicago, to her memorial service. In her home, while in prayer, she spoke again. In her broken English, with her strong Japanese accent, she said to me, *"Finally, you in my home."* Okasan, rest in peace.

~ SOULMATES ~

Soulmates appear in our lives on a variety of levels. Not only as a spouse or life partner, best friend or relative, a soulmate can be anyone in our environment that allows, or incites, spiritual transformation. He or she can be with us for a lifetime or for only a moment. Either way, it is a karmic link, created in other lifetimes, under other circumstances.

Because of the depth and intention of a soulmate relationship, no one else can provide this revolution, this learning, in quite the same way. When we meet, we may think it is for the first time but it is not. Buddhist philosophy holds that life is eternal, that connections are never broken, only suspended for a time. We will meet friend and antagonist alike, in lifetime after lifetime, to learn the lessons, make the changes, and accomplish the mission.

In appreciation for family, friends, and those who have caused me to expand. Thank you for our shared experiences.

Gwen, rest peacefully.

~ EPILOGUE ~

I continue to describe myself a novice, as life never sleeps. There is always someone else to meet, something new to learn. The sun will set. The moon will rise. Then, reverse. There is existence and simulated non-existence. Then, there is the realm of *spirit*, existing within us and outside of us, waiting for discovery.

Since my granddaughter's birth several years ago, there has been a hush in my home. Spirits appear infrequently. It could be, with her arrival, I am not as focused on them. New events constantly fill the time and space. But my vicarious legacy is highly perceptive. I hope that her spirit can grow exponentially, without limitations. I hope she can be free to live true to herself.

Stay conscious.

Also by D Tealer:
From My Point of View (2008)
i'm just sayin' (2012)

www.ingramcontent.com/pod-product-compliance
Lightning Source LLC
Chambersburg PA
CBHW031444040426
42444CB00007B/970